The Pursuit

The
Pursuit

Becoming
Christian
Leader

a
Business

How do you build an inspired brand?

A practical guide by **Adam C. Smith.**

The Pursuit
Becoming a Christian Business Leader

A product of Blue Creations

Find us on the world wide web at www.bluecreationsart.com
To report errors, please send a message to bluecreationsart@gmail.com

Scripture quotations are taken from the Holy Bible, New Living Translation, copyright © 1996, 2004, 2007, 2013, 2015 by Tyndale House Foundation. Used by permission of Tyndale House Publishers, Inc., Carol Stream, Illinois 60188. All rights reserved.

ISBN-13: 978-1-7348282-0-7

To my amazing wife Amanda who always believes in me

Preface

Thank you for picking up this book, cracking it open, and going on this adventure with me. This is my very first self-published book, and it was a labor of love. I wanted to create something that could be read quickly, applied immediately, and referred to continuously. My hope is that you can get through this book in a matter of a few hours and reap the benefits from it for the rest of your life.

Due to the widespread ability to self-publish our ideas, I no longer had any reason to keep these concepts on my hard drive or in my journal. I've shared these bits and pieces of wisdom that I've collected over the years with the people in my life, but this is the first time I've attempted to unite these thoughts into a useful guide. This book is filled with the advice I would give you in person if we both had plenty of time and plenty of coffee.

The hardest part of writing this book was deciding what to keep out of it. I had two false starts where I would get about 50,000 words in and realize that this wasn't headed in the right direction. This is the third version of what I've tried to articulate, and I believe I've been able to strip it down to its essentials.

As I was writing it for the third time, I finally had peace that I was on the right track. I do not think this book is "perfect", but I hope it's perfect for you. I invested a lot of time and money in learning these principles, and I invested about two years distilling them into this form for my audience. I hope you enjoy reading it, but I really hope that it blesses your life!

In His name,

- Adam

Contents

Let's go on an adventure...

Introduction

4 Take delight in the Lord,
   and he will give you your heart's desires.

- Psalm 37:4 NLT

I cried out to God one night in December of 2001 while I was locking up the used cars. I was working at Subaru as a salesperson and couch surfing at a friend's house. I had been evicted from my apartment a few weeks earlier for not being able to pay the rent. I felt deep fear and loneliness every day during that season of my life. I had heard about Jesus as a kid, but I didn't really know Him. I certainly wasn't following Him.

Instead, I was trying to do everything the world told me would bring me satisfaction in life, but the more I participated in it, the more pain I experienced. I was on the edge where either my life would have to change or I would start to consider ending it. I was filled with pain, depression, and guilt from all the choices I made the year before. I had alienated most of the people who actually cared about me for the temporary enjoyment of strangers in my party life. It was a really bad trade. So I made a deal with God (who I wasn't completely sure existed or cared about me) that I would change if He would only help me. To my surprise, God showed up three days later.

He brought my ex back to me in a seemingly random parking lot encounter who had been living out of state. We got back together and got married. We started attending a church where I heard the gospel preached in its pure simplicity, and I knew that I needed to put my trust in Jesus who freely forgave sinners. From that moment on, God began to put everything back together. He got me a new job at a local Nissan dealership a few months after our first child was born.

In those first few years of following Jesus, I was trying very hard to figure out what it meant to live my new life as a Christian. As a car salesman, I was trying to figure out how to sell more cars so I could feed my family. The advice I got from both groups seemed to conflict. Some Christians told me it was impossible to be a Christian and stay in sales. On the other side, a few of my non-Christian coworkers would occasionally mock my faith making me question whether or not I was welcome there anymore. Fortunately, one of my managers and a few of my coworkers were also Christians, and they were always willing to answer my questions. As of 2004, I started to experience success in my work selling over 30 new Nissans per month, and I started to experience God's love and peace in my life.

My quest for truth had begun! Over the past twenty years, I've read hundreds of great books on business from people of all different belief systems and backgrounds. I've earned my MBA, and I had a lot of wonderful professors. I've listened to lots of video content and went to multiple seminars. I've had some very influential mentors. I've done my very best to learn as much as possible about business.

As a new believer, I read multiple translations of the Bible in the first year, went to Bible study every week, asked questions, read a few other Christian books, and visited different churches. I was trying to understand both topics better, but I was also trying to resolve this tension I was feeling between faith and work. I didn't know where I belonged. I felt found and lost at the same time. Every once in awhile, I would find a Christian author writing about business; guys like Zig Ziglar and John Maxwell. Those books were very helpful early on in showing me that there were Christians in sales. However, it would take me several more years and many more experiences before I would mature in my understanding of both business and my faith.

There are a lot of books out there that will sell you the *secret formula* for how to become a millionaire. This isn't one of those kinds of books. The reality is that only God knows how much money He is going to entrust to you during your life. This book may help you learn how to earn a good living for yourself, or you may become one of the world's next billionaires. I have no idea what your future holds or how many dollars God will let you manage in this life. Whatever that number becomes, I pray that you steward it well. Instead of trying to achieve a certain level of income, my advice would be to just go to work, work hard, and expect that God will raise that number over time as you demonstrate your ability to manage it. This book will help prepare you to do that.

I love to help Christians succeed in business. In this book, I rely as much as possible on scripture and borrow from the best business strategies that I know. I want to help you integrate good business strategy with what it means to follow Jesus. I want to give my readers the one book I wished I would have had when I was in my early twenties. My goal is that this book will give you confidence to go out and build the business God is leading you to build.

If you're anything like me in your quest for answers, then you probably understand the struggle in trying to find resources on this topic. You go to Barnes and Noble or the library, and there are only a few Christian authors talking about business. You go on YouTube, and it's hard to determine the good information from the bad. You talk to other Christians about business, and you recognize the very different approaches that exist for how we should live in this world. You search for a Christian business leader podcast, and you realize there aren't very many Christian leaders talking about business. You begin to realize how large of a void we have in this subject area. You also start to hear Christian pastors admit how poorly of a job the Church has done over the years helping those who are called to business feel affirmed in it.

These are some of the reasons why I wrote this book. I felt like there are a lot of people like you who could benefit from a book like this, and I decided to self-publish one that contained the lessons I've learned over the past twenty years. I believe that if you work through this book taking each topic to heart and applying it to your life, then you will be able to take advantage of these principles much sooner than I was. I've benefitted from so many other authors, and I am a product of all of their wisdom. My hope is to contribute something just as helpful through this book.

The economy has shifted so quickly during the first twenty years of the 21st century that some old jobs are being eliminated while new jobs and businesses are being invented. It's important that we are equipped to succeed in this environment. I am writing this book to those of you who are in a position of influence over the business you work in. You may be a founder, owner, manager, or sales professional.

I believe every Christian in business will be blessed by reading the first part of this book. Some of you may not find as much value as we move into parts two and three depending on your current role, because you don't have control over some of the things I'll cover. If that's you, then the main benefit is that you'll have a good understanding of what it takes to build and grow a successful business. This will prepare you for higher level roles so that you'll know what to do when you get there.

Before I wrote this book, I made a list of the benefits I wanted to deliver to my readers. Here's the list I came up with:

Confidence - I want to help you with some of your fears, doubt, discouragement, and uncertainty as you navigate what it means to be a Christian business leader. I want you to have peace that you're exactly where God wants you to be; wherever that is for you right now.

Clarity - I want to avoid confusion, distraction, and information overload. That's why I kept it brief and avoided telling very many personal stories. I want you to see everything presented as one congruent whole that is easy to understand.

Direction - I want to help you if you feel disorganized, lost, or inconsistent in your work so you can move forward. It's easy to feel stuck in a situation, but this book could be your way out.

Saved Time and Effort - I want to help you improve the quality of your work, enhance your learning curve, and get great results faster. There are a lot of things that can get in the way of getting work done.

Improved Results - I want to help those of you who are struggling, living paycheck to paycheck, or feeling stalled in your career. I've been there; more than once. I believe I know how to help you move forward and achieve the results you want to see.

I've written this book in three separate parts that build on each other. While you can read the book in a matter of hours, you cannot apply it all quite that fast. These lessons will build on themselves and make more sense as you experience them over time. Keep this book close at hand, and refer to it over the years as you progress.

Part one is designed to help you build a solid foundation as a Christian who is living the mission out in the business community. Part two helps you begin to build the framework for a successful business. Part three is geared towards helping that business to grow. All of these parts are designed to help you and your business become healthy and strong.

So who am I and why should you listen to me? I'll give you the short version. I grew up poor. All I knew after high school was that I didn't want to be poor any longer. I grew up with a passion for art, but I was too afraid to risk ending up as a starving artist. I also enjoyed business, and I saw sales as my way out. That's what gave me the initial drive to work hard and learn more, and I eventually found success. Becoming very good in sales led to becoming a sales manager, and my experience in sales management led to my first role in retail management.

I've achieved progressive successes over the years and worked for a few really great companies including Starbucks and Target. I earned my Bachelor's degree in Media Arts and Animation prior to earning my MBA. In the background of all of those things, I was actively serving in the church and learning more about God as I was discerning my call to full-time ministry. This has given me a very unique perspective on this dilemma that people like us face.

However, that's just about me. I believe the real proof that these concepts work is that I've used them to help others succeed, too. As a manager and business leader, I had the privilege of helping several people develop and promote to higher levels of leadership. I wasn't able to explicity share my faith in those situations, but the principles were present. As a small business owner and consultant, I've helped several small businesses clarify their brands and increase their sales. As a Christian leader in my community, I know the struggles believers face on a daily basis, and I know how faithful our God is as He helps us walk through them. I've been able to help counsel lots of people and encourage each of them to trust God even when things seemed dire.

I'm a person just like you who has faced and overcome adversity in business as I sought to understand what it meant to follow Jesus. I have my story to share, and I know which principles have worked for me. The information in this book are all the practices I've integrated into my own life. My hope is that these practices benefit you just as much as they still benefit me.

How should you approach a book like this? I recommend that you start with prayer. God is the source of all wisdom, and He is always available! Further, I want you to consider the necessity of prayer for the Christian business leader. There are so many things that you need to pray for, so the practice of being in communication with the Father is simply a great way to start each day. He is there to direct your steps better than any book or success guru could ever do.

For example, you have your own life to pray for and potentially a family. You have to earn an income. You have to deal with emotions that change constantly. You have lots to learn and practice in your field. You have customers to serve. You may have employees you lead. You may have risk to manage. You have the community and government to deal with. You have changing economic conditions and advancing technologies. I could keep going, but I think you get the point. As if that weren't enough, we also have a real spiritual enemy. What else popped into your mind as you were reading that list of things you should pray about? I hope you can see that prayer is not just a luxury; it's a necessity.

Obviously, you can't spend every minute of every day on your knees in your prayer closet, so what do you do? My recommendation is to learn how to abide in prayer. There are moments of the day where praying on your knees is wonderful. However, there are many other ways to pray, and you can maintain open communication with God throughout the day. For example, you can pray privately in your own mind or jot down little notes of inspiration and praise. Whatever you do, don't try to go through this life journey without God's guidance and wisdom. He has given you the Holy Spirit for a reason. Imagine having access to every answer for every problem you will ever face. As a believer, you have this access. God created everything that exists, so He has a pretty solid grasp on how everything works. He has the answers you need.

Other than prayer, the other thing many of us need to understand is that we have permission as Christians to succeed in business. As a new believer, I was trying to understand money and greed, because I wanted to honor God while staying in business. I wanted to know that I had permission to be who God created me to be, so I want you to know that you have this permission, too. That brings us to our first Big Idea.

Big Idea:

You have permission to be who God created you to be.

Part 1 | Build the Foundation

	LOVE		
	WORK	GENEROSITY	
PART 1: BUILD THE FOUNDATION	GIFTS	PROBLEMS	SERVICE
	MISSION	CALLING	MINISTRY
	GOD		

CH 1 | God

14 Look, the highest heavens and the earth and everything in it all belong to the Lord your God.

- Deuteronomy 10:14 NLT

Before we start building a business or a framework for a business, we need to lay a solid foundation. As a Christian, your foundation is Christ. In part one, I am going to help you lay a foundation built on rock instead of sinking sand. We're going to cover ten chapters together, each dealing with a very important theological topic. There may be other topics you want to include in your foundation which is fine, but I find these ten to work very well when developing Christian business leaders. Let's get started!

Who do you Report to?

Just about everyone you know has to work to support themselves and their families. Just about everyone you know has a direct supervisor. We are expected to do a good job, and we give an account to that supervisor for our results. If you're a Christian, then God is the one you ultimately report to. God still wants you to obey your human supervisors, but there may be some situations where what God wants you to do trumps what your human supervisors want you to do. For example, you may have a manager that instructs you to tel a small lie to a customer to get them to buy your product. What do you do? You may feel like you are stuck between competing desires, and you'll need to rely on God's guidance and wisdom to navigate those times.

The Kingdom of God

As a Christian, you are part of God's Kingdom. As a citizen of the Kingdom and a child of the King, your business becomes one way in which you serve others. As we seek the Kingdom, God promises to meet all our needs. Notice that I said needs and not wants. God is not a genie in a bottle that grants us wishes. That would put us on the throne, and that throne is not ours to sit on. God is on the

14

throne, and our good God is our provider. In order to serve the right King, we need to understand which Kingdom we really belong to. If you were born again, then you are part of God's Kingdom.

Missing the Mark

As humans, we've all done things that are good as well as things that are evil. You may not see it as evil, but God's standard of holiness is higher than we tend to think it is. One definition of evil is the things we do that oppose God's ways. This makes us all lawbreakers, or sinners. To sin means to miss the mark, and every human being misses the mark. Most people begin to hate evil when they see how destructive it is to ourselves and others; even if they don't call it "sin". We see people call evil and injustice out all the time on social media. God hates sin, because sin is completely contrary to his good, perfect, and holy nature.

Unfortunately, every business leader has sinned and hurt their neighbors in some way. It might have been small and unintentional. In more extreme cases, their evil was so great a documentary may have been made about them and put on Netflix. These business leaders face some form of earthly justice when they sin such as fines or prison. For example, the media always seems to have a current news story about a corrupt corporation. We may not be engaging in unethical behavior at a high level like those notorious CEOs; we may simply be treating our employees poorly. Regardless of how good or bad we think we are, God shows us that we all miss the mark in some way.

The Bible tells us that God won't let evil go on forever. There will be a day when He finally puts a stop to it. Between now and then, the Good News is that Jesus came to save us and help us change by transforming our hearts and minds. When we believe in Him and turn towards His way of living our lives, He gives us the desire and power to love people well.

His love changes how we run our businesses, treat our employees, customers, and the community around us. As believers, we should make every effort to work towards good deeds that bless others and stop doing things that hurt our neighbors. Will you still mess up from time to time even as a believer? Yes, we will all make many mistakes. However, as you confess those things and turn from them, God is faithful to forgive you and give you another chance. There is no limit to the abundant grace of God.

Redefining Success

How do you define success? Who are some successful business leaders who come to mind? If a business makes a lot of money, stays in business for several decades, has a strong brand, and has a lot of happy employees and customers, then it is usually considered to be a successful business. If the business fails, then it is usually considered a failure. I would like to say that while this definition has some truth to it, for the Christian it isn't sufficient. First, we don't have control over the future. We don't have control over the market. We don't have complete control over whether or not the customer likes what we're selling. Also, there are many things that are profitable that aren't godly. Therefore, profitability cannot be the only measurement of success for the Christian business leader.

Here is a different definition of success that I would like you to consider:

[Success = Loving God + Loving People]

Sound familiar? It should! It's our greatest commandment! If you did a great job serving people through your business, even if it didn't work out perfectly, I still believe that Jesus would say to you, "Well done." It's not what you achieve that matters the most. God isn't commanding us to build earthly empires. He's not calling us to just do whatever makes us happiest. He's calling us to something far more important; to love God and love our neighbors. Without love, all the earthly success we could dream of wouldn't matter at all. This is a definition of success that you won't find in other business books. All other definitions that I have read seem to leave God out.

Let me affirm that I wouldn't have written this book if I didn't want you or your business to be as profitable as possible. I also want you to make a lot of money if that's God's will for your life. As a general rule, I also believe God wants you to succeed in what He has called you to do. Now, with all that said, I believe that God's definition of success may look different than we are taught in business school. I believe that if we love our neighbors through our businesses, we are successful regardless of the size of our business. This isn't permission to be lazy or chase failure. Instead, it's a mindset shift that allows you to focus on what matters the most in this life; especially in a time where everyone is trying to get you to only focus on yourself.

Put God First

If you are a Christian who is called to business, then you need to realize that money is not your Master. You belong to Jesus, and you should put God first in everything you do. The average American lives for about 80 years. We're only going to be on this planet a brief time compared to the scope of eternity. We need to stop worrying about some of the things that are temporary like how much money we made and redirect our focus towards the things that will last forever.

Here's an exercise you can do to check your heart. Put both hands out in front of you and open them with your palms facing up. Pretend you have all the money and fame you could ever want in your left hand, and you have God and everything He promises you in your right hand. While I believe that there are some famous wealthy Christians out there and having wealth isn't a problem in itself, let's pretend you could only have one. Which one would you cling to? I hope you chose God.

If you are having a hard time with that, then there might be a piece of you that's like the rich young ruler in the Scriptures. I don't know you, and I'm not your judge. I understand how hard that choice may feel. I spent a good number of years trying to serve both God and money, but when things got hard it was usually the money that I clung to. Even when that happened, God didn't give up on me. It took awhile for God to show me that even if I became as rich as Jeff Bezos or as powerful as the President of the USA, God could end my life at any time and in any way.

We are taught that money is security, but the only true security is God. We brought nothing into this world, and we can't bring anything with us when we die. All the riches in creation belong to God; how we handle money reveals what is in our hearts. If you still struggle with putting God first, my prayer for you would be that God helps you see money from the right perspective. Money doesn't last, and it's a horrible god. There's only one God that is worthy to be worshipped, and He was revealed to us through Jesus Christ.

Until you put God first, you can never operate your business the way He intends. Your love of money will always take your eyes off of what is truly important. That's why this had to be the first chapter in this book. There is no point in trying to help someone become a Christian business leader if they are not ready to put God first. But if you are, then you need to start with understanding that God owns everything in this world, and that includes your business. God will expect you to manage that business His way, and my goal in writing this book is to help you do that.

Big Idea:

God is the true owner of your business; your job is to manage it well.

CH 2 | Mission

43 But he replied, "I must preach the Good News of the Kingdom of God in other towns, too, because that is why I was sent."

- Luke 4:43 NLT

God's Mission

The American culture teaches that our purpose in life is to become rich, famous, and to pursue our own happiness. Unfortunately, this causes us to constantly compare ourselves to others, and we almost always end up feeling either superior or inadequate. Feelings of superiority can cause us to harm our neighbors. Feelings of inadequacy can cause us to harm ourselves. Neither of these things are good, so why do we live our lives this way? This reduces the purpose of our life to thinking we're either a winner or a loser; to either feeling temporarily happy or feeling completely hopeless. Instead, the Bible teaches us that God's purpose for us is so much better than that.

What is His purpose for us? God created us in His image for relationship with Him and with each other, but we separated ourselves from God by Adam's original sin in the Garden. The entire Bible is one story about God's redemptive plan for mankind and His future Kingdom. This is God's mission. This is what He is working out every day of our existence. Our job is to believe this Good News and receive it with joy! When we turn to Him and decide to live life His way, the Holy Spirit seals us and goes to work transforming us day by day so that we will live holy lives. We begin to reflect God's image to the world. God's purpose is to give us true life; both now and in eternity.

Being on the Mission

Once God saves you, He trains you up and sends you out to tell others the Good News about Jesus and God's Kingdom. As followers of Christ, we love all people and we share our story about what God has done in our life. Most of you do not need to quit your job to be on this mission with Jesus. In fact, your workplace and your community is exactly where you are meant to carry out this mission. When your alarm clock goes off this morning, you will get ready for work, eat your breakfast, complete your commute, and arrive at the office. You will have your schedule, tasks, and meetings that need to happen. The type of work you do doesn't change, but how you think about your work once you are mission-minded changes everything.

The Bigger Picture

It's important to understand this next statement I am about to make, so as you read it, think about it for just a moment before you continue reading. Here it is:

If you assume that there is no God, then there really isn't much purpose in our daily activities.

Our life would only consist of our childhood education and upbringing, roughly fifty years of work routines, some level of savings in our retirement account, and then we die. This mindset towards our careers is what causes so many humans to try and find meaning in things that cannot satisfy, and when they realize those things won't satisfy, it often leads them to become addicted, depressed, or suicidal. For when there seems to be no purpose in life itself, then there is no purpose in living it.

In contrast, when you look at life God's way, you will see your work differently. You will realize that the work God gave you is a gift and an opportunity to serve Him and others. God is not nearly as interested in how many widgets you sell as He is about using your life to help establish His Kingdom. We're not in our jobs just for the temporary things; He placed us there for the things that will last for eternity.

We're there for the people. Your company has a mission, but so does God. We need to honor our bosses and do great work for our companies, but our focus needs to remain on His mission.

How do we practically live this out? The first thing we do is put God in the center of our lives. God doesn't step into our mission; we decide to step into His. That is what helps us to shift our focus. The second heart shift we make is from working for what we can get to working for what we can give. This will focus our attention on the needs of the people around us. The third thing is we can actually practice what we preach. It's not enough to learn about service or kindness by reading the Bible; the Bible affirms that we need to act on it. We need to serve people and be a light.

We shift our focus from:

OUR MISSION to GOD'S MISSION

GETTING to GIVING

KNOWING to DOING

As you begin to truly love your coworkers and customers and build relationships with them, they will begin to feel God's love for them even if you never said a word about Jesus. That's why I don't worry about workplace policies getting in the way or specifically working for a Christian company. If Jesus lives in you and you reflect His love, you don't actually have to talk about Jesus in the workplace. You can be like Him instead while honoring your workplace policies.

Trust is built when people know you care about them and you keep your word. The trust and positive reputation you build with people is the foundation of relationships, and the relationships give you the opportunity to share your story about Jesus at some point with words. Can you see how your occupation has very little to do with your ability to be on the mission? This is something we can all do regardless of our occupation!

As you go to work each day, you and all the people around you will be working towards the company mission. Simultaneously, you as a Christian will also be working towards God's mission. It's not either or for you; it's both. You don't necessarily need to advertise that you're on God's mission; you just need to live it out. You also need to be patient, kind, and respectful of the people around you who don't know Jesus yet. Don't expect them to see work or life the same way you do. Just love everyone and earn a good reputation with all people. This is the first step in winning people to Christ.

Big Idea:

God's mission is saving His people and establishing His Kingdom.

CH 3 | Calling

28 And we know that God causes everything to work together for the good of those who love God and are called according to his purpose for them.

- Romans 8:28 NLT

Discovering Your Calling

Among Christians, the word *called* gets thrown around constantly. Understanding your calling may feel like a mystery at times. How do you know what God wants you to do with your life? Can you be called to the marketplace, or is the word calling reserved only for professional ministry leaders? God does not call people to do things that are against His standards, but just about every other job you can think of could be considered someone's calling. This definitely includes working in business.

Knowing if people can be called to the marketplace is easier to understand if you consider what God's mission is. I touched on this in the last chapter, but I'll unpack it a little more here. God uses your calling to accomplish His mission. God designed each human being with a unique set of interests and skills. He put you in a certain place at a certain time in history, and He helped you get the job you have. If you are good at accounting, for example, praise God! We need accountants in this world! More importantly, it's not an accident. God planned that and placed you where you're at for His mission.

Called to Be God's People

In your occupation, God wants you to do good work and be successful. This is how He provides for us and our families. It's just not the main reason He put you there. Regardless of what your job title and duties are, you are called to be part of God's Kingdom. The way you earn a paycheck may change over time, but your citizenship in the Kingdom never does. God put you wherever you are to be a light and demonstrate God's love for creation.

You will meet people that your pastor may never meet. Even if your workplace does not allow people to discuss their spiritual beliefs, you can still demonstrate them. You can love people, be generous, patient, kind, forgiving, and a hard worker. You can be their friend. You can be an ambassador for how good our God really is. Sometimes, you might even get a chance to share the reason for your hope. Can you imagine what would happen if Christians in every sector simply reflected who Jesus is in the way they treated others?

Called to the Marketplace

At the intersection of your passions, talents, and people's problems, you will often find your calling. The combination of those three areas provide clues. For those of you who are reading this book, that might be in the marketplace. Here's how you can start to figure that out.

1. Take a few minutes and think about what you're passionate about. Jot down some of those things.

2. Next, think about some of the things that you're good at. What comes to mind first?

3. Lastly, what kinds of problems do people have that you could solve? They don't always need to be huge problems. They might be as simple as providing your customers with a good cup of coffee.

What answers did you come up with? Can you see a connection between those three areas? Are you already in a place where you're fulfilling your calling, or do you think God may be preparing you for it?

Write Your Answers Here

1. Passions

2. Talents

3. Problems to Solve

There is one last point that I would like to bring up before we move on. The last piece of this puzzle is usually discovered through the affirmations of your community. People will call things out about you that you may not see yet; both affirming as well as critical feedback. The feedback may be a gift that others recognize in you, or it may be an area that you will need more training in before you can step into your calling. Either way, God can speak through the people in your life to affirm what is going on in your heart as it pertains to your calling. Whatever God has planned for you, I believe you will find it at some point. Just remember that all the things of this world are temporary, but the things we do for God's mission last forever.

Big Idea:

God uses your calling to accomplish His mission.

CH 4 | Ministry

6 In his grace, God has given us different gifts for doing certain things well. So if God has given you the ability to prophesy, speak out with as much faith as God has given you. 7 If your gift is serving others, serve them well. If you are a teacher, teach well. 8 If your gift is to encourage others, be encouraging. If it is giving, give generously. If God has given you leadership ability, take the responsibility seriously. And if you have a gift for showing kindness to others, do it gladly.

- Romans 12:6-8 NLT

You're in the Right Place

When the apostle Paul wrote about the spiritual gifts God gives us, it's true that they are to be used for various types of ministry in a church gathering. However, they were never meant to be limited to that. There is a difference between attending a church gathering and being the church. The church isn't the building or the service times. The church is the total assembly of believers functioning as the body of Christ with Jesus as the head throughout the world.

Jesus is always with His people. You can be the church in every square inch of God's creation, and that means ministry can happen in the marketplace. Ministry is ultimately about sharing your faith through both word and deed. Your ministry flows from your calling which is rooted in God's mission. The things you do for others is based on the things that God has prepared in advance for you to do. In other words, the place you do your vocational work is the place you will end up sharing your faith.

Be a Bright Light

You may be allowed to talk about God in the workplace, or you may have policies against it. In either situation, you are called to be a bright light. What does Jesus mean by being a light? He describes it as doing good deeds that everyone notices. Jesus did a lot of teaching and preaching, but Jesus did many other forms of ministry including healing people, feeding them, and listening to them. He met people's physical, spiritual, emotional, and even financial needs.

Everyone saw what He was doing and came to Him for help even though not everyone believed in Him as Lord.

I think that's important to understand so that we do not become discouraged in our ministry. This is the model He provided for us. He performed lots of miracles for all kinds of people knowing that it would result in only some people praising the Father. If Jesus taught us to love even our enemies, how do you think He wants us to treat everyone else in our communities?

Upside Down Kingdom

It's easy to only want to take care of ourselves and have other people serve us. Most of the thoughts we have each day are about ourselves. We all want to become great, but Jesus turned that upside down for His followers. He taught us that if you aspire to become the greatest in the Kingdom, you need to become like the least. He shifts the focus off of ourselves and onto how we can help others. Even though Jesus is the King of Kings, He decided to come to Earth as a servant. Even though He is the Master, He took the form of a slave and washed His disciples' feet.

He showed us that our lives are not supposed to be about what we can get; He showed us that the best blessing is found in our giving. Jesus is our model for how to live our lives, and He could have demonstrated anything to us. He could have sat on a throne and had everyone bring Him grapes like Caesar. Instead, He ministered to the broken and the hurting and sent us out to do the same. You will have the opportunity to serve the broken and the hurting through your business.

You just need to start seeing people as God sees them. Jesus spent time with all kinds of people and loved them, and God has no favorites. In God's eyes, everyone has equal value regardless of whether they currently worship Him or mock Him. In society, we want to sort people into classes. We often ignore the poor and see them as a nuisance, and we often show special treatment to the rich. Are not all made in God's image? Of course they are. Every human being that God made is precious to Him. That's why Jesus endured everything He went through. While we were His enemies, He died to save us. If that same love is in us, we won't treat people differently based on what they can do for us or how much we like them. Instead, we'll choose to love them all, because that is the right heart for ministry.

Big Idea:

Your ministry flows from your calling.

CH 5 | Gifts

10 God has given each of you a gift from his great variety of spiritual gifts. Use them well to serve one another.

- 1 Peter 4:10 NLT

Burying our Gifts

Are you using the gifts God has given you to help others, or are they sitting on the sidelines waiting to get in the game? It's very possible that God has given us a gift that we know is there, but for some reason we have buried it and refuse to use it. We may be envious of what others can do or have achieved and begin to think that who we are isn't enough. This can cause us to try to be something that we're not, and that can make us feel even more inadequate. As a good friend of mine once reminded me, "we can't wear someone else's armor." We need to be ourselves.

Seeing our Gifts as Valuable

In order to do our ministry well, we need to be able to appreciate how God designed us. One of the things I've done in my career is graphic design. I know that the things I designed for my clients had a desired function in mind, and I did everything I could to make sure the thing I designed functioned well. Things that are designed have certain capabilities but also many limitations. God has designed us the same way.

God calls us His masterpiece. He put careful thought into which gifts He would give us and which ones He would give to other people. His wisdom in this is that we would use these capabilities to minister to each other. If you decide to believe that your gift isn't important, then who is going to do your job for you? That's like saying, "I don't need a toaster, because I have a microwave." Have you ever tried to make toast in a microwave?

Whatever you have and wherever God has placed you, I believe that He has given you gifts for your ministry. Only you can do what you can do the way that you can do it, because that's how God made you. When you use your gift, other people benefit from it. The Bible lists helping as a spiritual gift. Helping someone doesn't feel very spiritual on the surface, but God calls it spiritual when it helps someone else know Him.

To refuse to see the value in the gift you have is insulting to the Giver. One reason people struggle with this is that other people may have ridiculed them for their gift and made them feel small. They aren't trying to insult God; they just feel inadequate about who they are. Instead of seeing it as valuable, they hid it. Whatever your particular reason is, let me encourage you to see that who you are and what you can do is very valuable to God and the people around you.

Developing Your Gifts

While God gives us gifts, almost all of them take some practice to become proficient. The gifts get stronger with use. For example, if you need to train your team today and it's one of the first times you've ever done it, then it may feel challenging even though God equipped you to do it. After you've conducted several training meetings, you will be much better at conducting them than you were in the beginning.

Having a gift is not a magic trick where everything is just easy for you. No one looks at a professional athlete and thinks they woke up one day and could play like that. They may have just had greater potential in that sport than the average person. They still had to work at developing that gift, so don't beat yourself up for not being automatically perfect. All you need to do is be willing to use your gifts to serve others in love. Developing our gifts is one of the ways we become better leaders. They also open the doors of opportunity to minister to others. Which gifts has God given you?

Big Idea:

God gives you the gifts you need for your ministry.

CH 6 | Problems

14 Our people must learn to do good by meeting the urgent needs of others; then they will not be unproductive.

- Titus 3:14 NLT

A World Full of Problems

Are you experiencing any problems right now in your business or your life? I think we all are to some degree. There are over seven billion people on this planet, and that adds up to a lot of problems. Some problems are bigger than others. While some people are trying to figure out which smart phone to purchase, other people are suffering from starvation and disease. As a Christian, we are empowered by God's Spirit to help other people with their problems regardless of how big or small they are. As a Christian business leader, someone in the world is going to need you today to help them solve their problem. You may be the only person God has called to do something about it. Are you ready?

Marketplace Problems

As Christians, Jesus commands us to do good deeds. In business, one of the ways we do good deeds is by using our gifts to solve marketplace problems. These may be internal problems where someone on the team needs help, or they may be the external needs of customers, vendors, shareholders, or other stakeholders in the community. You may also run into problems that are affecting your business like competition or new laws. You are going to run into a lot of different problems every single day. The key to handling these problems as a leader is thinking about how to do what is best for everyone, as much as possible.

I also want to point out that some people have problems that are unspoken. They may have come into your coffee shop for a cup of coffee, but their secret problem is they just got some bad news and are scared. As a Christian, our love for people gets them that cup of coffee, but it also gives them an encouraging smile that provides hope. Do you see how you can provide a good or service while simultaneously doing your ministry work?

The sweater I buy today from the department store won't matter very much in a few years, but the place I will spend all of eternity does. As you help me with my purchase, you have an opportunity to get to know me a little. If you remember my name the next time I see you, now we are acquaintances. We may run into each other somewhere and strike up a conversation. Now we're practically friends! If this continues, we may grab lunch together one day. After several lunches over several months or years, I would have gotten to know that you are a Christian. One day, I may finally ask you what that means, and you can tell me all about what Jesus has done for you. After I hear you tell me your story, I may begin to understand that I need Jesus, too. I may ask you to pray with me, and when you do, all of heaven throws a party. This all happened over a sweater, but it really happened because you saw your vocation as a chance to be on the mission.

That isn't my real story, but it could have been. All these temporary problems we have can bring believers into relationship with unbelievers and give us opportunities to share Christ in one way or another. God used my basketball coach to reach me. He may use a real estate agent to reach someone else. Since the beginning of time, the one problem that everyone has in the marketplace is that not everyone has trusted Jesus as their Lord and Savior...yet.

As an example, let me explain how God used basketball to reach me. I wasn't raised in a Christian home. I knew a little about Jesus from relatives, but we didn't go to church. Instead, my parents got divorced when I was in the 1st grade, and I experienced a lot of poverty and brokenness after that. I believe both of my parents were doing their best, but it wasn't easy growing up in those conditions. In the 10th grade, my basketball coach was a Young Life leader. We bonded over basketball, and he invited me to their small group and later to a summer camp. I didn't believe in Jesus right away, but I never forgot Steve's example as a Christian. I knew he cared about me, and I knew he loved Jesus. A few years later and after making a lot of mistakes, I finally realized I needed to trust Jesus just like Steve did. If I never met Steve, then God might have chosen to send someone else. However, that's not what happened. God used basketball to reach me. That's why we should never underestimate what God can do.

Solving Problems

Productive leaders and fruitful ministers have at least one thing in common; they tend to solve a lot of problems. There are going to be some that you can't solve, but don't beat yourself up. Problems provide you with an opportunity to serve regardless of the results. People appreciate your willingness to go the extra mile even when you don't always have a solution.

I know some people who wish their lives were problem free, and I understand why they feel this way. However, the book of James shows us that God allows some of these problems to happen to us for our good. Our problems may teach us to trust Him more, or they may give others opportunities to serve us so they can grow in their gifts. God uses trouble to test our faith, grow our endurance, develop our character, and prepare us for future challenges. While some problems may cause us to panic, I don't think God is ever truly worried about the outcome. God has His children in the palm of His hand, and nothing can separate us from Him. As a Christian business leader, we can put our confident trust in our Lord that He has given us everything we need to help others.

Big Idea:

You solve people's problems by using your gifts.

CH 7 | Service

45 For even the Son of Man came not to be served but to serve others and to give his life as a ransom for many.

- Mark 10:45 NLT

The Heart of Service

We solve people's problems through providing great service. However, there are a lot of times where people don't receive great service.

Do you view business ike it's a Chess game where there is a winner and a loser? When you close a big deal, do you have a sense of pride or gratitude? Have you noticed the connection between money and how it makes you feel? Our attitude towards money is reflected in the type of service we deliver.

Loving money causes us to serve people only when we want to get money from them. If they give us money, we treat them well. If they do not, they don't always get the best treatment. In contrast, loving God causes us to serve others out of an overflow of the love we've received from Him. This allows us to focus on others instead of just ourselves. When customers do business with you, do they know you care about them? Or do they feel like you only want their money?

Examples of Poor Service

In a world where there are online reviews for everything, it's easy to find examples of poor service. Here are a few things that frustrate customers:

- Incompetence
- Lack of empathy
- Having to repeat themselves
- Not getting their problems solved
- Waiting too long
- Being hard to contact
- Slow response times
- Being treated like a number
- Broken promises

Examples of Good Service

Here are some examples of things that customers appreciate:

- Smiling and learning their name
- Asking for feedback and listening
- Replacing something at no extra cost
- Sending thoughtful notes or gifts
- Tailoring the buying experience
- Sharing credible and important information
- Loyalty programs and rewards
- Going the extra mile
- Finding ways to improve their experience
- Responding to concerns quickly

The Problem is in our Hearts

When we look at the two lists, the big difference between the two is that the examples of good service indicate a desire to build a long term customer relationship. If you have fear, insecurity, pride, or arrogance in your heart, then it will be difficult to build long term customer relationships. Instead of seeing a human being in front of you, all your focus will be on what you can get from them. How you treat others reveals what is going on in your heart.

Early in my sales career, I was taught that most people only care about "what's in it for me". I think that is generally true, but God expects something different from His people. In the letter to the Philippians, Paul encourages the believers to think about other people's needs and not just their own. Stop trying to impress people, and start taking an interest in how you can help the people around you.

God Transforms our Hearts

How do we change our hearts? From my experience, I do not believe you can change your heart by working harder. Trying to fix yourself leaves you feeling one of two ways; you'll either feel superior to others or inadequate based on how things are going for you at that moment in time. Neither of these are helpful. Instead, you just need to ask God to change and heal your heart. Confess the areas of your heart that you know aren't right, and He will be faithful to help you change. You'll recognize that your grip on trying to get what you want loosens up, and you'll make a shift towards what you can give.

When you become a Christian, you are no longer the same. God begins to charge your heart. As He does this work in you, your faith starts to grow. As your faith grows, God gives you opportunities to do good deeds. In this way, taking action demonstrates the faith that we have. It shows us and the people around us that we have truly changed. As God changes our hearts, He works through all of us to change the world.

Service is our Way of Life

There are plenty of problems to solve and people to serve. Serving others well pleases God. It demonstrates your faith in a lot of different ways. It shows that your actions match your words. It shows that you recognize God will meet your needs and you don't have to worry about it. It shows that you have an eternal perspective on life instead of an unhealthy attachment to the things which will fade away. Also, you'll demonstrate your belief that your own happiness isn't the only important thing in the world.

Sometimes, we may have to do things that aren't easy on us in order to bring happiness to others. As a Christian business leader, service isn't something we do; it's a part of who we are becoming. Jesus didn't set us free just so we could go do anything we want. His purpose is that we would use our freedom to serve other people in love.

Big Idea:

We serve people when we help them solve their problems.

CH 8 | Work

6 Take a lesson from the ants, you lazybones.
 Learn from their ways and become wise!

7 Though they have no prince
 or governor or ruler to make them work,

8 they labor hard all summer,
 gathering food for the winter.

- Proverbs 6:6-8 NLT

Learning How to Work Hard

Everyone has a different level of laziness. Some people really do work hard most of the time, but I think most of us lean towards laziness by default. You may work harder at some things than others based on your interests, but I'm sure it isn't very difficult for you to think of an area in your business where you could be working harder. But why does this matter?

The reality is that most businesses fail due to incompetence. According to the U.S. Bureau of Labor Statistics, half of the businesses that start will fail within four years on average, and over 65% fail within ten years. As I mentioned in chapter 1, this doesn't always mean you failed in God's eyes if you served people well. However, if you failed because you were lazy, that's very different. Laziness prevents you from serving *anyone* well. Proverbs 13:4 states, "Lazy people want much but get little, but those who work hard will prosper and be satisfied."

As we are learning to work hard, we usually start with ourselves. After we have learned how to do good work, we may be given opportunities to lead others. We teach them what we learned and encourage them to work hard as well. If we do well in lower levels of leadership, we are often promoted to higher levels where we are leading the leaders. This allows us to multiply our efforts through others and have a greater impact for the Kingdom.

A Better Way to Work

Most organizational hierarchies seem to be shaped like pyramids, but is that the best way to work? God uses ants as an example. Ants are interesting creatures. Individually, they aren't very remarkable, but they can accomplish amazing things when they work together. Each ant goes about doing its own specialized work, and the whole colony benefits. What would your church or company look like if this is how everyone worked? Instead of having "bosses" over groups of people trying to force everyone to work hard, you would have "leaders" who were there to serve the people doing the work and solve some of their problems making their jobs easier.

This is what happens when everyone realizes that we're ultimately serving God. It takes hard work to serve others, but it's exactly what God wants from us. I know there are times that we need to wait on God to do only what He can do, but the people who usually say this often overlook all the Scriptures and examples of where hard work was modeled. We should be waiting on God as we're working.

Challenges with Work

Sometimes our problem isn't laziness. Sometimes we are workaholics. This other extreme is equally dangerous to us and the people in our lives. Work is important. The Bible has over 500 scriptures about work, and work is described as a gift from God. However, even God rested on the 7th day of the week.

All throughout the Old Testament, we see that God gave mankind the Sabbath which was a day of rest where they were commanded to stop thinking about work and remember their God. It was to be protected and considered holy. Jesus explained that the Sabbath was really a gift that was intended to benefit us. How does it benefit us? It causes us to regularly be reminded of who our God is so we won't be tempted to worship idols.

Working too hard is usually caused by an improper view of what you need to be doing. Is there an idol in your life like power, position, money, expectations, fear, insecurity, guilt, envy, or some other thing driving you to work too much? Did you know that working too hard can be a bad thing?

First, you put your own health at risk. How can you do the work God gives you if you wear out the body He has given you to do it with? Too much work has an impact on the quality of the nutrition, exercise, sleep, and spiritual rejuvenation we need to be our best selves. Jesus made time for all of these things. We should, too!

Another example is that it can affect our families. If God has blessed you with a spouse and/or children, it is sinful to neglect them. They have needs, too. Paul recognized that people with families were never as free to do ministry as single people, because they had other responsibilities to meet. There are certain jobs where the divorce rate is higher than other jobs due to the amount of time a spouse is separated from their families. How well can you minister to others when your own family is falling apart?

Lastly, working too much will get in the way of your relationship with God. It always does. God provides 7 days of provision for you in 6 days of work so you can take the 7th off to spend time with Him and those closest to you. Take your day off!

Workplace Excellence

It is a good goal to do your work with excellence and provide great service. Diligence is persistent excellence over time. Diligence leads to prosperity. This is accomplished by strengthening our gifts and working together as a team.

You can accomplish far more when everyone does their part than if you try to be Superman by yourself. Working with others is not easy; it takes effort and unity. But it's worth it!

Remember, you aren't just building a business or accumulating wealth; God is building His Kingdom through your service. Ten people each going in their own direction won't get very far. However, ten people working together and doing their own unique part can move mountains. These kinds of organizations are usually very successful, and think about the amount of influence you would have for the Kingdom!

That's what is at stake when we don't work the way God wants us to. When we're lazy, the people who need us don't get help. When we work too hard, the people closest to us don't get help. We need to follow God's schedule for work. The right people in the right roles, doing the right work, for the right people, with the right heart, for the right amount of time...these people can accomplish anything!

Big Idea:

It takes hard work to provide great service.

CH 9 | Generosity

10 For God is the one who provides the seed for the farmer and then bread to eat. In the same way, he will provide and increase your resources and then produce a great harvest of generosity in you.

- 2 Corinthians 9:10 NLT

The Ultimate Goal

There are a lot of people in the world of business that believe the ultimate goal in life is to become extremely wealthy. In the U.S.A., the place where there are more millionaires than anywhere else, the total number of them is just over 5% of the population. As for the number of billionaires in the U.S.A., it drops to .000186% of the population. In the world, there is only 1 billionaire for every 2.8 million people. Even if we just consider the millionaire population in the U.S.A., we see that 95% of the people aren't millionaires. Are they failures? Of course not.

However, since so many people think their identity is somehow linked to the amount of money they make, a lot of people end up feeling like a failure. They scratch and claw under the name of "hustle" to try and make it into that elite group. Most people don't make it, yet there are so many people trying to sell you the secrets of becoming rich. All your thoughts get funneled into this single direction, but even if you accomplish it, it never truly satisfies. For the Christian, your identity cannot be defined by your ranking on a list of the world's wealthiest people.

Identity in Christ

If your identity is tied to a number, then you will feel a need to protect that number. You'll forget that 80% of all the people on the planet live on less than $10 per day and that half live on less than $2.50 per day. That's at least 6 billion people living in extreme poverty at the $10 per day level. Since you believe that your worth comes from your wealth, very little of that money will be given to these people. After all, you have to protect your ranking, don't you? If your identity is about being a wealthy winner, then that makes their identity the poor losers, *right*?

We need to stop falling for that lie from the devil. If you belong to Jesus, here's who God says you are regardless of your income:

- We are children of God
- Made in His image
- Dearly loved
- Created for worship
- A chosen people
- Part of the body
- A special possession
- His masterpiece
- All on the same level
- Temple of the Holy Spirit
- A new creation
- Holy and blameless

God's Generosity Towards Us

Depending on how you interpret the role of tithes for the Christian, you may believe that God wants to take 10% of your money. That's a very poor way to see it. God doesn't need the money, and it's all His anyway. He doesn't want 10% of His money back; He wants 100% of your heart. It's your neighbor who needs the money. There isn't one thing we have that He hasn't given to us. Further, there isn't one thing He has withheld from us including His only Son. God is extremely generous towards us in so many ways, and He expects His children to be generous, too.

Our Response Should be Generosity

I hope your business becomes extremely successful. I really do! However, even if you aren't as successful as you might like, I pray that you become extremely generous with what you do have. In America, lots of people play the lottery hoping to get rich. We live in the richest country in the world, but we still think we're poor. The average household income in my area is about $55,000 per year. The other 80% of the world makes less than $3,600 per year with some making less than $300 per year. The reality is that we're already rich, and we don't even recognize it. If the person making $300 a year saw someone making $55,000 protesting about how little money they made, how do you think they'd feel about that?

If you are a Christian business leader, then you should thank God every single day for what He has given you. Further, you should figure out how to be generous with your time, your money, and your talent. As you are faithful in your work, God will bless your business so you can be generous. If you are fortunate enough to have employees, you should be generous towards them. Also, you should teach them to be generous to your customers.

Everyone in the community knows which businesses are generous, and they are grateful for them. Generosity isn't about giving what you don't have out of guilt and putting your business at risk. Generosity simply says, "I'll give you whatever I can, because I care about you." This makes God very happy, because God loves a cheerful giver!

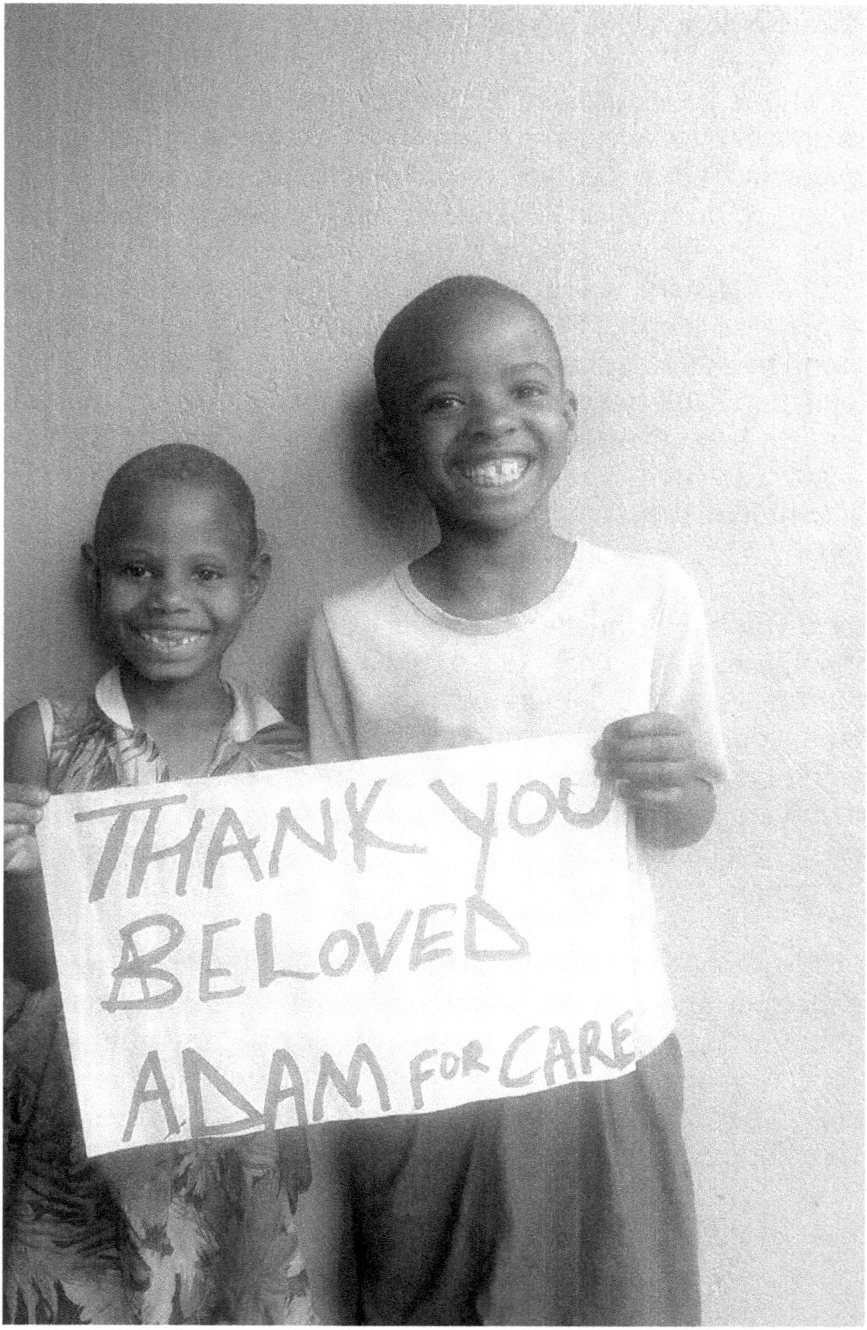
THANK YOU
BELOVED
ADAM FOR CARE

Big Idea:

We are able to be generous, because God blesses our work.

CH 10 | Love

13 For you have been called to live in freedom, my brothers and sisters. But don't use your freedom to satisfy your sinful nature. Instead, use your freedom to serve one another in love.

- Galatians 5:13 NLT

Learning to Lead People

Before you ever lead people, you need to learn how to lead yourself. You need to learn how to be responsible and give your full effort. You need to understand the job you do before you can teach others. The best way to learn to lead people happens before you get a title. Leadership is about influence; not just your position in an organization. By this definition, *everyone* is a leader.

In the workplace, you learn to lead others by the influence you gain with them. Some of the ways you earn this influence is through the example you set, the way you serve others, and the encouragement you give. Many people view leadership as being in a position to tell others what to do. They fail to realize that their ability to get people to take action is based more on their influence than on their positional power. If you cannot gain influence with people, you will not be their leader very long.

Learning to Lead with Love

Influencing people without caring about them is called manipulation. You'll only view people as a means to an end or like pawns on a chessboard. Although Jesus was worthy of being served, He didn't come to Earth for that. He wasn't feeling neglected up in heaven and decide to come down in a human suit and beg us to worship Him. Jesus came to serve because He loves us, and He is our perfect model in leadership.

In order to lead people well, you have to love them. I'm not talking about romantic love; save that for your spouse. I'm talking about a love that truly wants what is best for the other person. If God has entrusted you with a position as

70

a leader of people, then you need to understand that they aren't really there for you. You are there for them, and they are there for the customer. If you get that order right, then you can become a great leader.

Learning How to Love

You may understand why this is important, but you may struggle to actually do it. How can you learn to love people when you don't *feel* like it? The only way I know of is asking God to change your heart. If we agree that we're born with a sinful nature, then we know we tend to care far more about our own happiness than the happiness of others. There's a part of us that is inherently selfish, and one of the first words every child learns is "mine".

The biggest miracles I've witnessed God do is to change people's hearts. He can turn selfish people into generous people. Loving others doesn't mean you have to hate yourself. Love simply means that you're willing to take the low road when you have the opportunity to give someone else the higher one. You can't give someone something that you don't have. But when you receive God's love and grace in your life, it becomes much easier to pour that love and grace into other people's lives. Jesus filling our hearts until they overflow with pure, living water is what gives us the ability to genuinely love others.

GOD
CAN
GROW
OUR
HEARTS

Love is the Greatest

Why is love so important in leadership? The reality is that you could take all the management classes you want, have all the answers, and have big visions and clever strategies, but if you don't understand that loving people is the real task at hand, then you will have gained nothing. The purpose of our lives is about far more than just routines, schedules, execution, or accumulation.

Love puts God first. God is love. Love is what powers the mission. Love helps us understand our calling and do our ministry. Love inspires us to use our gifts to solve people's problems. Love provides great service and works extremely hard. Love overflows from our heart into generosity towards others. These are the things that lay a solid foundation for the Christian business leader. Working only for money is empty and uncertain. Instead, commit to the Lord, and your plans will succeed! Paul taught us in 1 Corinthians 13 that, "There are three things that will endure - faith, hope, and love - and the greatest of these is love." Love is the key to a solid foundation in your life, in your ministry, and in your business.

Big Idea:

Love is the motivation for our generosity.

Part 1 | Build the Foundation

God | God is the true owner of your business; your job is to manage it well.

Mission | God's mission is saving His people and establishing His Kingdom.

Calling | God uses your calling to accomplish His mission.

Ministry | Your ministry flows from your calling.

Gifts | God gives you the gifts you need for your ministry.

Problems | You solve people's problems by using your gifts.

Service | We serve people when we help them solve their problems.

Work | It takes hard work to provide great service.

Generosity | We are able to be generous, because God blesses our work.

Love | Love is the motivation for our generosity.

Part 2 | Build the Framework

PART 2: BUILD THE FRAMEWORK		

RESULTS	MONEY	
SCHEDULE	EXECUTION	
LEADERSHIP	MANAGEMENT	
GOALS		
BUSINESS MODEL		
LOVE		
WORK	GENEROSITY	
GIFTS	PROBLEMS	SERVICE
MISSION	CALLING	MINISTRY
GOD		

PART 2:
BUILD THE
FRAMEWORK

PART 1:
BUILD THE
FOUNDATION

CH 11 | Business Model

3 Commit your actions to the Lord, and your plans will succeed.

- Proverbs 16:3 NLT

Now that we have worked to strengthen your spiritual foundation in Part 1, we are going to transition into how to understand the structure of your business here in Part 2. If you are reading this book, there's a high probability that you either work in a business now or you are considering launching a new one. I will not get too deep into the weeds on any one particular subject, and I will not cover every subject that could be discussed in business. There's plenty of great information out there already. The purpose of Part 2 is not to be exhaustive. The purpose is to get you thinking about some of the higher level components that make your business actually work. My goal is to help you be Christ-focused in your approach while equipping you with proven business strategy. In Part 3, we will start talking about how to grow the business.

In this chapter, I want you to start jotting down notes and ideas when you read these questions. We will be using this information later in the book, so it's best not to skip this step. There are a lot of different business models, but they all share a similar structure that includes value propositions, customer segments, customer relationships, distribution channels, a revenue model, partnerships, priorities, resources, and expenses. I want you to take some time to analyze your business model and think about why your business works. Next, think about areas you might want to improve. Most importantly, I want you to think about how you can serve the people God brings to you through your business.

As I've mentioned before, you will either look at your business in light of only what you can get from it or in light of how you can serve God through it. One attitude puts self first while the latter puts people first. This chapter will take you on a tour through your business model. Answering the following questions will help you look at your business as a whole so you can understand it better. Let's begin!

Value Propositions | What are you selling?

A value proposition is a marketing statement that explains the benefits of your products or services to your customers, the problems they solve, and how your company delivers value better than your competition. Value propositions are connected to your mission statement, because they explain what you intend to deliver. They can be as simple as three words, or they can be a well crafted sentence. In order to craft your value propositions, you need to know your position in the market. How do you stand out?

You will usually have different value propositions for each of your main products and services. Also, value propositions are tailored to your customer segments since they satisfy unique wants and needs. Look at each of your products and services, and write a value proposition for that customer segment.

Customer Segments | Who are you selling to?

A customer segment describes who you are trying to deliver value to. It includes demographic and psychographic information. It describes exactly how many people could benefit from the product or service, and it should examine if this market is expected to grow or decline. In a business, it's very important and efficient to know who you are trying to target so that you can streamline your efforts. Who would you rather invest your time and money on? People who have a 90% chance of needing and wanting your product, or a 10% chance of needing and wanting it (assuming the market was the same size)?

Are you in a business to consumer or business to business model? If you're in a business to business model, what types of industries need what you have? Which businesses are able to afford what you have? Where is there unmet need? What problems do businesses have that you can solve? The answers to these types of questions will help you figure out where you should deploy your resources.

Customer Relationships | How do you connect with customers?

Customer relationships deal with how you are going to connect with your customer segments. What does this relationship look like, and what is your strategy for starting these conversations? How do they expect to hear from you? How expensive is it to communicate that way? Do they always need to talk to a person or would a F.A.Q. page suffice? Understanding these relationships are important for both acquiring and retaining your customers.

Distribution Channels | How do customers purchase your products and services?

How do you get your product or service into their hands? The traditional distribution channels included up to four groups of people; producers, wholesalers, retailers, and consumers. Depending on the business you're in, you may have more complicated channels that include agents, resellers, brokers, telemarketers, and many other ways of reaching the end user. As a general rule, complicated distribution channels are the most expensive to operate. Ideally, every business would simply set up a website and sell directly to the consumer. However, some business models simply cannot operate that way.

It's important to know what options are available to you, the costs involved, the benefits of each, and their drawbacks. You may need to use a few different distribution channels or find ways of integrating the ones you already use. For example, it may be beneficial to create partnerships with other businesses who have developed a large audience. You would make less money per unit sold, but it might help you sell millions of products to customers that you couldn't reach on your own.

Revenue Model | How will you generate revenue?

What is it that people are actually willing to pay for? How do they pay and what are their preferences? How much money do you make from each revenue stream? As you start to track all the different ways you make money in your business, one thing you may find is that some revenue streams are not profitable. In those cases, you need to figure out why that is. If you determine that it can and should be fixed due to its importance for your business, then all you need to do is take action on it. If you find that it's actually hurting you more than it could ever help you, then you may decide to eliminate it from your mix. Over time, you'll begin to understand the core components of your business, and you can try adding and deleting revenue streams to see what is profitable for you.

Partnerships | Who helps you deliver value to customers?

Very few businesses do every part of the business by themselves. In most cases, in order to bring value to the market, businesses help each other in some way. You need to understand your place in the distribution channel. Are you the manufacturer, wholesaler, retailer, or some other key player? Who else is involved?

It's important that you understand which partnerships are vital for the success of your business, and you need to do everything you can to make sure these partnerships are going well. If they aren't, you either need to figure out how to work together better or find a different partnership. Each key partnership will involve some exchange of value. You will either be buying from the one above you or selling to the one below you in the chain. Are these the right partners for you? Having the right partners can make a huge difference in the success of your business.

Priorities | What needs to happen?

Every business has a set of activities that must be accomplished in each area for the business to work. Some of these activities are vital and some may be a waste of time and resources. If you list out everything that could be done in the operation of your business, then you could sort that list into what your key priorities are from most important to least important. Is there waste on that list that can be eliminated? Is there an action that needs to be taken that has been neglected?

In your business, what are all the things that have to happen for it to work? What are the top three priorities in your business that need to be improved? Start there. The activities you write down that are vital to the operation of your business can help you identify if you have any gaps. Understanding them will empower you to give the right direction to your team.

Resources | What must you invest in?

There are key resources in each area of our business that enable us to deliver value to our customers. They could be the goods or materials. They could be machinery or technology. These resources might be human, intellectual, or financial. You will need to make a list of what resources are needed in order to make your business work. Taking inventory of what you need will help you understand what you do not need. These areas of investment that are unnecessary are usually waste and should probably be eliminated.

No business has unlimited cash, so we need clarity around which business investments are vital. Having the resources you need will make you a more effective operator.

Expenses | What will it all cost?

Your competitive strategy will help determine some of your cost structure. Which partnerships, priorities, and resources cost the most? Which are the most vital? On a P & L, you will deal with both fixed and variable costs. You need to understand which areas you have more control over than others. Other concepts related to your cost structure are economies of scale and economies of scope. Both of these deal with how much production is ideal to keep costs down. There are times where higher levels of production actually hurt profitability due to the increased cost of delivering them.

In order for a business to be profitable, it can only do a few things. It can increase profit margin, increase sales, or lower its costs. You should do all three, but you can only lower your costs so much. You need to accept that there will always be some sort of cost involved in operating your business, and you need to know the difference between the costs that are vital and the ones that can be lowered or eliminated. You should seek to lower your costs as much as possible without affecting the business. Most importantly, be on guard against greed in this area. Don't put profits ahead of people; conduct your business fairly. Don't seek to cut costs so much that you start hurting the very people who are there to help you be successful.

Products and Services

What are the specific products and services your business offers? Large businesses may have thousands of products. If this is the case, try to think of things in terms of categories. Make a list of them and try to write down how they fit into your overall business model. Do you know why you are offering each of them? Do you know how they connect to your mission?

New business owners will often try to sell too many things which is problematic. They overcomplicate their business model in an attempt to create more revenue streams. They turn themselves into a generalist who is spread too thin instead of specializing in what they do best. They take on unnecessary costs that do not enhance their customers' experience. Adding unproductive things may actually be working against them. If that describes your situation, then they may need to be eliminated to free up resources for the things you are best at delivering. In this way, it's actually possible to be more productive by doing less.

Speaking Points

How will you communicate value to your customers? How will you let the public know what's new and exciting at your business? What will you say? You should write these things down. These kinds of statements become your elevator pitch, taglines, and slogans, and they will assist you in your sales and advertising efforts.

Products and services are often multi-faceted. Each customer may appreciate something different about them. You should know the top reasons why your customers might like them, and you should know the one unique selling proposition that makes what you sell better than your competition's product. Communication is made up of a few key building blocks; text, pictures, and sounds are the typical ones. How will you translate the benefits of your products and services into ways your audience can receive?

Big Idea:

Good leaders understand how their business works.

CH 12 | Goals

21 You can make many plans, but the Lord's purpose will prevail.

- Proverbs 19:21 NLT

The Importance of Goals

If God is in control, should we even bother setting goals? The book of Proverbs as well as other passages in the Bible certainly support the idea that setting goals is important. To move forward with the vision God has given us, we should take the time to set goals in order to focus our energy and resources. This is part of good stewardship.

Also, spend some time in prayer. We often have no problem seeking information from books, consultants, or Google. In contrast, God knows all things and owns all things, but we don't usually seek direction from Him. If God created this whole universe, doesn't that seem like something we should do? Before each day gets started, make sure you start your day in the most important meeting! Meet with God for a few minutes however you like to pray, and search His mind. Dedicate time each day to be in the presence of God, and He will show you what to do.

Strategic Plan

A strategic plan is a way to set goals and develop a plan to achieve them. It helps an organization make decisions on how resources should be allocated to accomplish the mission and vision of the organization. A strategic plan usually involves goals, objectives, and tasks. Goals are things you work towards as you seek to accomplish your mission. You don't need to write a lot of goals. In fact, sometimes 1 to 3 goals is sufficient. Each goal may have a few different objectives that need to be reached in order to accomplish the goal. An objective is helpful for getting more clarity around the steps needed to achieve a goal. You can take this one step further and add a few tasks for each objective. Critical tasks would be specific things that need to happen by a specific time to achieve the objective.

There is no perfect number for how many goals, objectives, and task you should create. The "right" number is the number that allows you to achieve your mission. Use as many or as few as you want.

SMART Goals

How do you write them in a way that is helpful to communicate with everyone on the team? That's where SMART goals come into play. This is a framework for how to write goals, objectives, and tasks. Good written goals have these five qualities in common. This will help take your ideas and focus them into something you can take action on.

Specific. If a goal is too vague, then you haven't thought about it enough. Being specific is like naming what you want to have happen. It has an implication that your goal includes sufficient detail. If other people read it, they should know exactly what you're working towards.

Measurable. Some things are easier to measure than others. In order to commit to your goal, you need to pick a measurement that enables you to know when you've achieved it.

Assignable. Who is going to do it? Is it something that only you can do, or is this something a person on your team will accomplish? You may even consider using some type of independent contractor to get work done.

Realistic. You should absolutely dream big, but it does you no good to pick a goal that you do not believe you can achieve. Most goals are achieved step by step. The one caveat I will add here is that God will sometimes give us a vision for a goal that we think is completely impossible. Our job in this scenario is obedience. While we may think something is impossible, all things are possible with God. God will bring it about in His time.

Time-based. People do not set deadlines for the same reason they do not set measurable goals. They are afraid of failure. However, it should be easy to set a deadline for your goal if it is something that you really want to see happen. Why wouldn't you want to achieve it as fast as possible? You can do this! If it's helpful, you may need to break the goal down into a few objectives each with their own deadline. Get to work on your SMART goal and accomplish it. Celebrate the win, and get busy setting the next goal. If you don't set a deadline, then you will probably procrastinate and eventually give up on it.

Examples of SMART Goals

"Hire a personal trainer to help me lose thirty pounds through exercise and improved nutrition over the next twelve months."

"Find ten new clients that I do design projects for in the next 90 days."

"Hire a roofing company to put a new roof on my home before September."

"Find 10 volunteers to help me host a charity event to collect coats and backpacks for kids within the next 6 weeks."

God Owns the Outcomes

Fear of failure is pretty common to both individuals and organizations. We are afraid we won't get what we want or need. We may not feel worthy to have anything good happen to us. We may feel guilty for dreaming big dreams based on our perspective of God. Despite all of these fears and insecurities, let me just say that the results we have are all ultimately up to God. Apart from Him, we can do nothing.

God is a good and loving Father, and He has wisdom in all the situations He allows us to experience. Only God knows how things will end up, so we don't have to worry about that. Our job is obedience. Since God is good, we can trust Him. It's really as simple as that. We need to move in the direction He is pointing and be patient as we work towards accomplishing our mission.

We may not see the results we hope for in the first year. However, if we continue to seek God's will, listen to His voice, stay connected to Him, and apply our full effort towards the work, then I believe the things God is calling us to will be accomplished. God made the heavens and the earth and everything in it. Is anything too hard for God?

Big Idea:

God wants you to set goals, but He owns the outcomes.

CH 13 | Leadership

26 But among you it will be different. Those who are the greatest among you should take the lowest rank, and the leader should be like a servant.

- Luke 22:26 NLT

The Need for Leadership

Why does God appoint some people to be leaders? Why can't we all just be on the same level with no one leading us other than Jesus? I think the answer to this has a lot to do with what the true purpose of leadership is. The reality is that all of us are leaders in some way.

In the Kingdom of God, leaders are the ones that serve the people in their care through guiding, equipping, empowering, comforting, correcting and protecting. Leaders use their wisdom and understanding to make decisions in accordance with God's will. If your reason for wanting to be a leader is about money and power, then you probably won't be a very good leader. You will look at the people on your team as a means to an end. To put it bluntly, you'll use people.

Your job as a leader is to help your people become who God created them to be. You do this through building authentic relationships. Most of them are probably there because they would rather have a job than start their own business at this time. In order to meet their needs, they know they need to trade their time, skills, and effort for a wage. At some level, they probably believe in the mission of the organization and the type of work they do or they would work someplace else.

Everyone that you lead is different, and God has a plan for each one of their lives. Your job is to simply help them take their own next step. There will be some people who will go from being an average worker to a model employee. There will be others that you will help develop for a promotion. There will be a few that you serve by releasing them to work somewhere else. You will get to be their leader

94

for different amounts of time. As you work towards serving the needs of your people, they will be working to serve the needs of your customers. If you take the time to serve them well, then they will be empowered to serve your customers well.

We need great leaders in our lives to help us become better. Also, every person on a team has something valuable to contribute that makes the whole organization stronger. A good leader can bring all these people together and influence them to move in a unified direction towards the accomplishment of a shared mission. If we didn't have leaders and every single person was trying to work independently of each other, then I don't think any of us would get our needs met. The economy works best when people work together for the production and consumption of goods and services.

Leadership Development

How can we turn our leadership potential into leadership ability? We are all works in progress. Take an inventory of your strengths and opportunities to improve. Your next step will be unique to you. Ask God to make your next step crystal clear. What is the one strength you should leverage more to help your organization? What is the one opportunity to improve that would make the biggest impact in your effectiveness as a leader? If you need some help with this, then chat with your supervisor or a trusted mentor. Knowing the answers to these two questions will help you set some goals for your own leadership development.

Traits of a Servant Leader

- **Vision** - you need to know and communicate where you are leading people.
- **Accountability** - you own your choices, tell the truth, meet your responsibilities, don't make excuses, and never blame others.
- **Team Player** - you do your part and help your team knowing that the team comes first.
- **Communication** - you communicate well, frequently, with integrity, and tailored to the right audience in various forms of communication.
- **Encouraging** - people want to be around you, because they know you help them be their best selves.
- **Execution** - you know how to get things done as a team, in the best manner possible, and you strive for results.
- **Relationships** - people matter to you and you work towards trying to get along well with all kinds of people.
- **Empathy** - you are able to understand how people feel and show compassion when needed.
- **Creative** - you look at problems with curiosity and are able to find new solutions.
- **Decisive** - you know how to do your best to take the knowledge and experience you have, and using God's guidance, make decisions in a timely manner.
- **Humble** - no matter how much success God brings you, you never forget that God is the one deserving of all praise.

The Holy Spirit is constantly working to refine us, and being faithful to obey what the Spirit is revealing to us is how we grow. Improving our leadership starts with a willingness to change. Be faithfully obedient to become a great leader in each moment of each day using everything God provides, and I believe that in time, you will become a person of great influence.

The Responsibility of Leadership

Stewardship of everything God gives us comes with a great responsibility. If you can recognize that God gave you everything you have and that apart from Him you could do nothing, then you will start to understand the responsibility that comes along with leadership. If you are faithful with what God gives you, then He will often give you more. If you prove to be unfaithful with it, then God may take it from you. This is a consequence; it's the way the LORD lovingly disciplines us.

God gives us power to lead, and He takes this very seriously since it impacts everyone in our sphere in some way. We need to feel the gravity of that. He doesn't give it to us because we deserve it. He gives it to us for His purposes and due to His grace. Humility is the posture each one of us needs to take as we wake up each day and go to work leading others. The people God has blessed with great ability, resources, and finances have a great responsibility to help those who have been given less.

Big Idea:

Being a leader is a great responsibility.

CH 14 | Management

2 Now, a person who is put in charge as a manager must be faithful.

- 1 Corinthians 4:2 NLT

Stewardship

Since the beginning, management of the world God created has been one of the key things humans were designed to do. As Christians, we think of management in terms of stewardship. Stewardship is a word that means supervising or taking care of things that have been entrusted to us. We steward each thing we're given for a different length of time. Before we can become a good steward, we need to be aware of the things God has entrusted to us. This includes money and the people we lead, but stewardship is much broader and encompasses every aspect of our lives.

God owns everything. He is the owner; we are the managers. He gives you a body, abilities, time, opportunities, resources, your health and the air you breathe, and people to serve in the business you manage. He gives it to you and then watches to see what you're going to do with it. If you've been called to business, then you are going to need to learn how to be a great manager.

The Management Cycle

There are five steps that make up this cycle: Planning, Staffing, Organizing, Directing, and Controlling. You always start with Planning and work through the steps to Controlling, and then the cycle repeats over and over again. The Management Cycle puts the Strategic Plan into motion. Let's take a brief look at each one of these steps.

Planning. Planning involves looking at the current state of your business, comparing that to your goals, and choosing what you are going to focus on as a priority. You will begin to create an action plan that outlines what must happen to achieve the desired result. You may need to break these steps down into smaller steps depending on its complexity. You'll need to take some time to figure out what resources will need to be used to achieve it. Like you learned in setting goals, you'll need to decide how to measure it and give it a deadline. This step answers the question, what are we going to do?

Staffing. Staffing is the next step, and this step answers the question, who is going to do it? Some of you may not have any employees, but that doesn't necessarily mean you have to do everything yourself. You could choose to outsource tasks to freelancers or another business. If you do have employees, then you need to make sure you have enough of the right kinds of talented people available to do the work. There are times where you may want to accomplish a big goal and you don't have enough employees. One of the things you'll need to do is to get fully staffed and trained, and this needs to be included in the action plan.

Organizing. In this step, you answer the question, how are we going to do it? You start by dividing up the tasks that need to be accomplished by each person or department. As you do this, you will start to design the structure in the organization for how everything will get done. This step puts you a lot closer to accomplishing the goal, because you can start to visualize what could happen if everything went as planned. This sets up a chain of reporting relationships where everyone works together to accomplish the goal.

Directing. This step asks the question, who do I need to talk to? As a leader, you use your influence to communicate, motivate, and coordinate. You take time to communicate with each person involved on your team, and they take it to their teams. You motivate your team to work together to accomplish the goal and get their buy-in. You coordinate all the activities that need to be done according to a schedule. You do all these things and more with the goal of getting the work done.

Controlling. It asks the question, how well are we doing? As the work is happening, the leaders are looking at the results and comparing them against your goals. They check in with the teams to see how things are going and if there's anything they can do to support the people doing the work. They manage the performance through both recognition and improving performance as needed. You'll either be meeting the expectation, surpassing it, or you'll be falling behind. If you find yourself falling behind, then you need to figure out what needs to be done to get back on track. At the end of the time period, you analyze the results and go right back into the Planning step for the next cycle.

Management Skills

Inside each one of these areas are a number of different management skills that must be used to accomplish the management cycle. A good manager can set goals, delegate, perform the hiring process, create a culture that fosters retention, manage their time, build teams, provide coaching and appraisal of employee performance, handle problem employees, deal with crises, execute strategy, understand budgets, and read financial reporting. These are just a few of the skills we need to be able to perform each day to manage our businesses.

How do we learn all these skills? Formal education is

helpful, but we can learn them little by little over time as we're faced with the normal flow of daily business. You should spend time at the end of each day reflecting on what you learned and writing down those notes. You should set aside time to train and research management topics and strategies. As we improve our management skills, we will begin to see improvements in how well our management cycle runs.

Making Improvements

We're not security guards. We aren't supposed to simply protect our resources. While we have a responsibility to watch over the things in our care, we should also seek to increase the resources we manage by making continuous improvements. Making improvements makes us more efficient, effective, and able to help more people. The two main keys to making improvements are knowing what you want to have happen next time and being honest with yourself about where you're currently at. One little change at a time taken over a period of time can radically transform the future of your business.

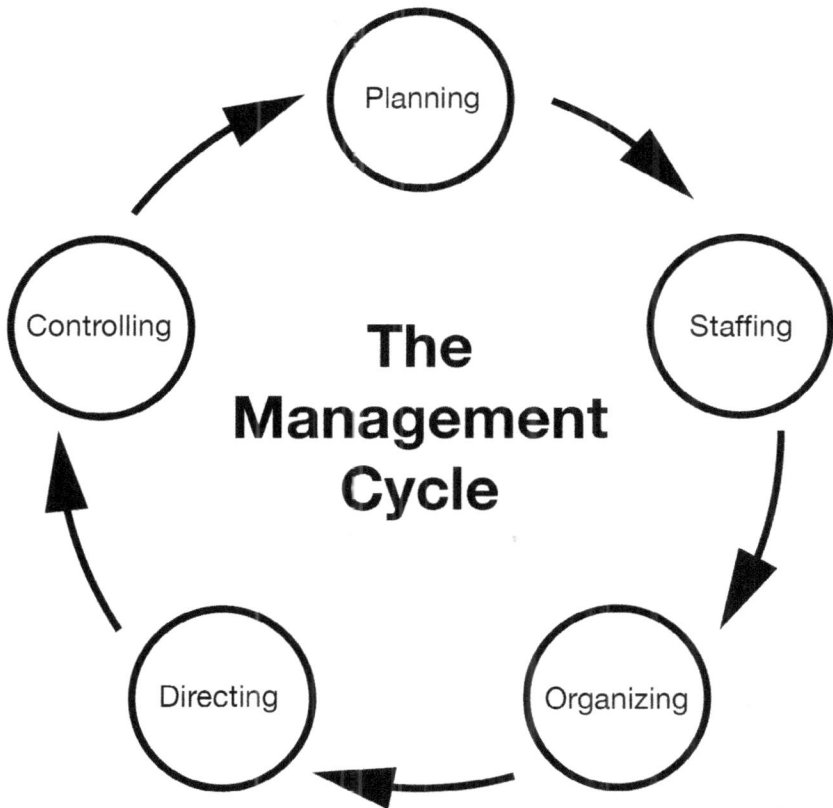

Planning

Controlling

Staffing

The Management Cycle

Directing

Organizing

Think Long Term

While we must learn to depend on God's daily direction and provision in our lives, it is also important to look up and out to where you are headed. Short-term thinking, hasty decisions, or trying to take shortcuts almost always ends badly. Managing your business this way may feel expedient in the moment, but wise managers will make decisions that will play out better in the long run.

As Christian business leaders, we are commanded to be faithful. We should be making decisions not simply in light of our businesses but in light of eternity. Our highest goal should be to one day hear Jesus say, "Well done, good and faithful servant." If we start with the end in mind, then we will tend to make much better management decisions.

Having a long term mindset will require diligence. Diligence is a word used to explain hard work and care provided over a long period of time. Learning how to use the management cycle, developing management skills, and doing the right thing long term each day of our lives requires diligence. Managing your business faithfully by being a good steward will lead you to become successful in the work God has prepared for you to do, and you will be able to enjoy both the temporary rewards as well as the eternal ones.

Big Idea:

Managing a business requires diligence.

CH 15 | Schedule

5 Live wisely among those who are not believers, and make the most of every opportunity.

- Colossians 4:5 NLT

Managing Time

Every single moment we have is a gift. God invented time, and He gives it to us in the form of a life. We all have 24 hours in each day regardless of which country we live in. No one gets any more or any less. We know that time is precious. This applies to the time we spend at work. Working off of a realistic schedule is one of the most important things you can do to manage your time well. This teaches you that you are going to have to prioritize. There are always plenty of things that could be done with your time, but there isn't always enough time to do everything. If you don't schedule your time, then you will end up making random decisions about what happens each day. You might forget to do the things that are actually important.

We will always be more efficient when we are operating in our gifts. Go all in on your top strengths and get help in the other areas. That way you can spend the right amount of time in each area of your life. You should make a list of all the things that you need to do and prioritize that list. Map out each thing on a calendar including time with family, friends, church, volunteering, personal development, your health, and rest. Stick to that plan with diligence, and I believe it will make a huge difference in your life.

A schedule is like a budget for your time. You decide in advance how you are going to spend it, and you do your best to stick to the plan. When interruptions happen, you handle them and get right back on schedule. Lastly, learn how to say "no" to the things that aren't important for your life so you have more time for the things that are important.

Personal Schedule

God worked six days and rested one, and I believe it's the right example to follow. Life isn't just about work. There are several things in your personal life that you need to schedule. These include:

- Time to be with God each day.
- Your family schedule.
- Date night with your spouse.
- Going to the gym or getting exercise.
- Preparing healthy meals.
- Getting enough sleep.
- Time for hobbies and pursuing interests.
- Hanging out with friends.
- Your small group.
- Your kid's extracurricular activities.
- Household management.
- Grocery shopping.
- Taking care of your pets.
- Family vacations.
- Visiting your extended family.
- Managing personal investments.
- Rest.

If your personal life falls apart due to neglect, will your work life really matter to you that much? Your personal life is very connected to your work life. They affect each other in major ways, and they need to be in some kind of balance. It's between you, the Lord, and your family on how you decide to spend your time, but I hope that you see how important it is to schedule the things in your personal life. Scheduling helps you establish guardrails on the parts of your schedule that need to be protected.

Work Schedule

When you're at work, there are a lot of things that need to be scheduled to be done by each person. Here are just a few of them:

- Operational routines.
- Managing employees.
- Executing your workload.
- Freight flow.
- Meetings.
- Appointments.
- Cleaning and maintenance.
- Various assessments.
- Doing the management cycle.
- Serving customers.
- Completing transactions.
- Promoting your business.
- Opening and closing the store.
- Handling signage and price changes.
- Answering the phone and responding to emails.
- Training.

There are some things that are not productive and may need to be eliminated from your schedule. They waste time and hinder your results. Show up on time for work each day, work your plan, give your full effort, and make sure you take at least one day off. Managing your schedule well will almost always double your productivity.

Scheduling Effectively

How can you write effective schedules for your team? Here are a few tips:

- Understand your actual workload before you write your schedule.
- Write down everything that needs to be done and then prioritize the list.
- Know your peak times and staff them accordingly.
- Look at future projects and forecast the number of hired employees you will need.
- Pay attention to approved time off and vacation requests.
- Try to make sure that your team is getting the right amount of hours they need to live on.
- Invest enough payroll hours into your schedule to prevent missed sales.
- Be realistic about your schedule by creating some padding.
- Know the timing of your vendors, contractors, or other partners who impact the schedule.
- Have a second set of eyes take a look to see if they spot any gaps.
- Do your best to write it well the first time, but manage it each day to stick to your budget.

Writing effective schedules for yourself, your business, and your team is both an art and a science. An effective schedule can help you maximize your sales, and poorly written schedules will significantly impact the success of your business. As you develop wisdom in each area of your life regarding how to plan your time, you will find yourself being more productive than you ever thought possible.

Rest

As business leaders, many of us struggle with the concept of rest. God gave us the Sabbath as a gift. God rested on the 7th day. Jesus withdrew to lonely places to spend time with the Father. Rest for the Christian should be considered sacred and just as important to our lives as the time we're working. If you never give yourself regular time to rest, how effective do you think you'll be long term? How good will your relationships be? How will your health hold up? As for stress, how will you manage it if you never slow down? You may feel guilty for resting, but you really shouldn't.

God wants us to love Him with all our heart, mind, soul, and strength. Rest has benefits in every one of those areas. In terms of strength, the physical benefits are reduced stress, opportunities for exercise, reduced heart problems, boosted immune system, better sleep, and it can literally extend your life. In terms of your heart and mind, the emotional and intellectual benefits are increased mental energy, creativity, productivity, focus, memory, satisfaction, joy, and peace of mind. As for your soul, God provides intimacy, engagement, relationship, presence, reminders of His grace, gratitude, renewed strength, and inspiration.

All these benefits come from rest. When we do not rest, we usually experience the opposite of those things. Why do you think people take a sabbatical? Regardless of whether or not people know Jesus, as humans we understand how important it is to take a sabbatical when we can. This is by God's design. Therefore, as much as we want to be productive and do good work, putting planned rest in our schedule is one of the most productive things we can do.

REST.

Big Idea:

The right schedule includes your work, personal life, and rest.

CH 16 | Execution

4 Pay careful attention to your own work, for then you will get the satisfaction of a job well done, and you won't need to compare yourself to anyone else.

- Galatians 6:4 NLT

Managing Your Numbers

The best plans on the planet are worthless unless someone takes action. The first thing you need to do to execute well is know your numbers and make adjustments to your activities as needed. In business, there are a few things other than time that you need to manage. Here are a few of them:

Revenue. It's important to have sales goals that are both realistic and profitable. What are the activities that must happen in order to achieve your revenue target?

Metrics. The things you should track depend on the type of business you're in. In sales, you track things like closing percentage, proposals presented, demonstrations, presentations, initial consultations, and the number of prospects in your pipeline. As a manager of a retail business, there are lots of different metrics for each business function including logistics, human resources, setting planograms, putting up signage, guest services, cashier transactions, food costs, and protecting against theft.

Cost of Goods Sold. You may be a manager of a retail business and people farther up in the corporation were the ones who negotiated the final price of the items you sell. The cost of those goods are set, and you can't do anything about that. However, you can make an impact in other areas including good inventory management and preventing shrink. If you are in a role where you have more control over the costs of the product, you'll want to find ways to reduce those costs. You can work out better terms with vendors or manufacturers by buying larger quantities, you can reduce packaging expenses with better design, and you can keep R & D costs down by making products simpler.

Labor Expense. This is one of the most expensive resources you'll have, but it is also one of the most important. You will have to balance minimizing your labor expense while simultaneously seeking to pay your employees well. Companies that take great care of their people are usually more successful, so don't shortcut this area. Profit should never be more important than doing the right things for your people.

Operational Expenses. These include your building, utilities, furniture, wifi, food supplies, paper supplies, decoration, and a myriad of other expenses that it takes to run your operation. There are also all the operational costs that happen behind the scenes like training and marketing. Businesses do not have unlimited funds at their disposal, so they need to make wise choices on what they purchase and what not to purchase. Some of this information should be shared with your team so they understand how their performance affects the bigger picture.

Investments and Finances. On a cash flow statement, you'll find expenses from operating, investing, and financing activities. Investing activities deal with the business investments you make such as buying an asset, any loans you have, and any payments related to purchasing investments. Financing activities deal with sources of cash going in or out of your business. They include things like issuing debt or equity, payments to shareholders, buying back stock, and paying back loans.

The Big 3 Financial Statements to Know

You should look at your reports on a regular basis so you always know how things are going. Here are some of the most important reports every business should have. You'll want to study these in more depth, but this is an overview.

Balance Sheet - This statement shows the financial status of a business at a specific point in time. The statement shows what you own (assets) and how much you owe (liabilities), as well as the amount invested in the business (equity). Remember, Assets = Liabilities + Equity.

Statement of Cash Flows - This statement describes the cash flows in and out of your organization. Its focus is on the types of activities that create and use cash, which are operations, investments, and financing.

Profit and Loss Statement - summarizes the revenues, costs, and expenses incurred during a specified period, usually a fiscal quarter or year.

Getting Things Done

When planning and setting goals, your job is to think about the highest value use of each resource you have, create the plan, and then you simply go get the work done! You execute on your plans in the Directing step of the management cycle. This s where the bulk of your team's time should be spent each week. All the other steps are important, but only some of the activities you do generate the revenue in your business. You need to make sure those activities happen.

Getting things done is simple, but it isn't always easy. There are many things that can hinder our work that we need to be aware of. Overcoming these things will help you and your team be more productive.

- **Our Emotions** - fear, frustration, anger, or other negative feelings that distract us.
- **Reduced Effort** - some days we have to battle laziness or apathy.
- **Procrastination** - it may be boredom or lack of discipline.
- **Gossiping** - we may find ourselves becoming nosy or complaining.
- **Being Off Routines** - we fail to plan or fail to look at our plan, and we lose productivity.

Training for Success

Sharpening an ax before you chop wood is very wise. It makes the task easier and faster. That's why it pays to invest in training. Learning is a lifelong process. God is constantly preparing us. There's always more to learn, and learning is how we grow and tackle harder challenges. Part of the learning process involves practice and sometimes even failing. No one is perfect, and we need to learn how to fail fast by realizing that most failures are just part of the learning process.

We need to build training into our schedules. We need time to learn new practices, and we need time to work on those practices. Some companies offer occasional training opportunities, but these should just be supplemental to your own training. Depending on your role, you will want to identify the areas of your job where you want to improve. As the leader, you should also help your team learn how to build training routines into their lives and even offer some regular training through your workplace. Also, it's extremely helpful to have coaches. If the best professional athletes in the world have them, then why should it be any different for the rest of us?

Jesus trained His disciples every day for three years before sending them out to do greater things. How much are you training for your compnay mission? How well are you training the people on your team? If everyone on your team improved their productivity by even ten percent, would this make a difference in how your organization executes? Of course it would! Training is what helps us reduce the time it takes to complete an activity from an hour to possibly only ten minutes. Training will help you maximize your execution and accomplish your goals faster.

Tools for Success

Technology has provided us with a lot of different tools that are designed to help with efficiency and productivity. These can be very helpful for small business owners. For example, approximately eighty percent of the registered businesses in Washington State (my home state) are one-person operations. These owners all wear multiple hats, and many of them struggle with getting everything done.

This is where automation can provide us with some relief and free us up to do other things with our time. One of the most common examples of automation is marketing software. There are a lot of great tools out there that integrate with each other, and they can automate a lot of different tasks that we would have to do manually.

Another great tool is your iPhone with free apps like Lists. You can use Siri to capture notes and convert spoken words to text. The camera can be used to convert photos to PDFs. It also has the ability to produce nearly all the content you need for your social media channels. Other smart phones have similar capabilities.

The basic purpose of any tool is to help you get work done easier. Having the right tools and knowing how to use them makes you more proficient at your craft. Think about the tools you use and write a short description of how each tool helps you. After you've done this, think about any problems you have that a new tool could help you solve. Or, is there an area where a better tool could replace one of the tools you currently use?

Communication

Mastering communication will make your organization more productive. One of the challenges to communication is that there are usually a lot of things that need to be communicated, and there are a lot of people to be communicated with. There are different ways we send messages, and some messages need to be sent multiple times. Getting great results often depends on having great communication.

Communicating effectively through your verbal, written, and nonverbal methods takes knowledge and practice. There are a lot of different dimensions to it. This skill is one of the things that separate the good leaders from the great ones. Further, being able to communicate effectively is usually one of the things that help people get promoted to higher levels of leadership. If you want your results to improve, it's worth investing some time improving these vital skills.

The last thing I will mention regarding communication is that your entire team has a role in it. For example, it is true that your marketing department will create some great slogans for your ads, but your frontline employees need to communicate the same brand message to the people they serve. Don't forget to communicate about communication!

Everyone Plays

Lastly, another ingredient to successful execution is getting everyone to do their part of the work. We see this in sports. The best team is the one where everyone is unified and does their job well. Those kinds of teams are the ones that win and are fun to be on.

Yet many teams have people on them who really don't want to be there. There are many reasons for this. They may have been excited at one point and became discouraged over time due to poor leadership. They may have faked some excitement in the interview simply because they needed a job. They may have just been a bad hire for the position. Regardless of the reason, this type of employee either needs to buy-in and do their part or they will eventually need to be let go. It is your responsibility to support them so that they really want to be a part of what you're doing.

Studies show that the majority of people in the United States are either not engaged, or are actively disengaged from their work. Can your company deliver great work when more than half of the team doesn't really want to be there? The answer is no. You may be able to accomplish mediocre work, but you'll never do great things without unity.

You need to get good at both of these tasks; hiring and firing. You need to create a culture where you slow down enough to hire well, you set proper expectations in the beginning, you have a zero-tolerance policy for things that are toxic, and you act swiftly when people do things that break unity. The good news is that when you build a culture like that, you will usually attract high-quality people that want to work in an environment like that.

In most companies, you are going to work with a diverse set of people. While you are living out the bigger mission God gives His people, just know that in this chapter I am specifically referring to your company mission. As a leader in your business, your goal is to do your best to get everyone united around this shared company mission. If you lead well and develop unity on the team, then you will start to see some great results!

Big Idea:

The best results come when everyone is united around the company mission.

CH 17 | Results

23 Work brings profit, but mere talk leads to poverty!

- Proverbs 14:23 NLT

Managing Results

Now that the work has been done, you need to step back and look at your results. How did you do? Where can you make improvements?

As a warning, you can't manage your results the right way unless you realize God is your provider. In terms of church growth, Paul made a point of telling the church in Corinth that it is God who makes things grow. He knew that he and Apollos had to do the work, but God was the one who made things happen. If you don't see how that same truth applies to your business, there's a good chance you'll either become prideful or fearful depending on your results.

If your business is booming and you don't recognize God, you'll walk around with a chip on your shoulder and start judging the "underperformers". Conversely, if you are struggling, you'll start to feel inadequate and incapable of seeing how things can get better. There's a third option. If we will simply focus on managing well, we don't really need to worry about the results. Our job is to step out in faith and do our best work serving others in every circumstance we face. God's job is to bring the results you need. You do your job, and let God do His.

Now that we've addressed the heart, the things that need to be paid attention to are the key drivers of your business. You may only be responsible for a single department, but that department will have some things to measure. For each key driver, you'll want to track things for a few months to be able to come up with some averages. You use your inputs (the activities you do) and outputs (the results you get) to determine your next level of inputs needed to achieve your goal.

Managing results for yourself is one thing, but managing results through others takes a very different skill set. The first takes applied skill and effort; the second takes influence. It's really the same process in both of those scenarios, but leading people requires you to increase your communication and help your employees be successful. You'll need to communicate expectations, give direction, provide training, provide on the job coaching, and provide performance evaluations. Employees need to be celebrated when they're doing a great job, but they also need to hear truth when their performance needs to improve.

Current State

Where do we start? In order to manage your results, you need to understand where you currently are. It's helpful to give your business a thorough review in all of the areas that relate to your key drivers or key performance indicators. You'll need to have a willingness to be honest and accountable for where you're at so you can improve. It does no good to act like everything is fine when it isn't. It might make you feel better temporarily, but you'll be looking at the same problem later when things are worse.

These notes that you capture on a review of your business and by looking at reports gives you a snapshot of the current state of your business. You'll usually find areas where things are going great, and you'll have some areas that obviously need to improve. This is a part of the Controlling step that rolls into the Planning step of your next Management Cycle. You'll want to share this feedback with the team, provide recognition to the employees who are doing great, and have follow up conversations with employees who need additional support.

Goal State

After you've defined the current state of your business, you need to figure out where God is leading your business. You need to set some new short-term goals. A goal state is how everything would look if everything you wanted to happen actually happened. You could also think of this as a desired future state of your business.

Larger businesses will usually set these for your store or department, or your direct supervisor will usually partner with you and guide you to the goal state that is appropriate for that time. If you are the owner, you need to discern what you believe God wants to see happen or refer back to the goals you set earlier. Either way, you need to look at each area that needs to be improved and make a decision about how you want it to be once it's fixed.

My recommendation would be to choose up to three of your top areas of improvement and start there. Next to each current state item, you should write down what your goal state is. You use this information in your Planning step, and then you start working the rest of the Management Cycle.

Identifying Gaps

What are the things between your current state and your goal state that need to change? How do you discover these gaps? One thing you can do is to conduct an audit for an aspect of the business. You can look at things like safety, customer service, sales, freight flow, food standards, or any other topic.

Audits require having a standard for how things should be. In an audit, you simply investigate the things that need to be checked out by walking an area of your business, analyzing related reports, and asking questions of employees working in that area. You record your findings, and you score them according to your ideal standard. This will provide you with a benchmark that can be used to measure future audits against. Some audits reveal issues that need to be addressed immediately, and others reveal metrics that are below standard.

Another thing you can do to identify gaps is to use benchmarks from other stores or the industry you're in to help you figure out how you're doing. If ten other stores like yours are all performing in a similar range and you are well below that number, then that may give you some insights into how you're actually performing. You need to make sure you're doing your best to avoid comparing apples to oranges, and this may be very challenging. Making unfair comparisons can be misleading. However, if all your other data points to the same problem including this type of comparison, it may warrant further investigation and improvement.

Asking team members who work in the area and have been with the company for a sufficient length of time is very helpful. You can always find people who are invested in their jobs and want to do well, and they will know how to find the pain points in a work center. They will usually have better ideas than you do, because they deal with it every day.

Peer reviews can be extremely helpful. You can send a trusted colleague into your business like a secret shopper. Teams will often work differently when they know their boss isn't there. Even if your team is great, every manager I have worked with had different strengths and could spot different opportunities to improve. Surrounding yourself with wise counselors who are knowledgable in an area can help you achieve your goal state much faster.

Driving Change

After you decide what needs to be fixed, you will need to start implementing change. Some changes feel overwhelming and impossible, but just know that change can happen. You build a wall brick by brick; not all at once. Looking at the big problem as one thing may feel intimidating, but focusing on just the one simple next action you need to take gets you on the road to achieving the goal. Driving change is less intimidating when you look at things as a progression of several small wins.

Most of the success stories we know about came after a long period of struggle. If God has given you a vision of what He wants you to do with your life, then you can't give up just because success doesn't come right away. You need to persevere. It may take longer than you want, but you can still get there if it's God's will.

The other problem you may have is that you feel like you're constantly going in circles. A part of you wants to change. You're actually working hard and trying not to procrastinate, but you find yourself continuing to have to start over. This can take a few different forms.

One example is where you think you have fixed a problem permanently but then it shows up again. You do the same thing, it goes away for awhile, but then it comes back. What's happening here? The answer is simple; you're fixing the wrong problem. If we don't find the root cause, then it's very possible we'll find ourselves with a "boomerang" problem. It does you no good fixing the wrong problem over and over again. To get past it, you need to figure out what is actually happening.

The next step after Planning is Staffing. Staffing addresses who is on your team and who will be assigned to perform a task or lead a project. Job descriptions help with this problem of assigning tasks to people who will be responsible for them. Most job descriptions have some level of flex space built into them for miscellaneous tasks. Certain tasks or projects will usually need to be assigned to specific individuals on your team in order to get the work done.

It's possible that the problem you face is that you don't have any employees to get all the work done that you want. There are millions of overwhelmed solopreneurs today in the USA. If you're one of them, you may have to choose to do less or delegate tasks to an independent contractor. There are lots of people in the world looking for "gigs" (one-time jobs to do) related to a certain skill. Regardless of the size of your team, make sure you follow up to ensure the work gets done. Inspect what you expect. This is how progress happens.

Managing Performance

Don't judge yourself too harshly if you start slow, and don't get too excited if you're way ahead of where you expected to be. Remember, God owns the results. Your job is to take the journey. With that said, you're probably going to have to manage the performance of your team along the way. You'll need to give praise when it's due as well as correction. Don't save it up and unload it all at one time. Instead, let it be part of your everyday conversations.

When people are doing well, let them know how much

you appreciate them. When things need some adjustment, give them the feedback they need to make changes. Recognition is the fuel that most people run on. If a month goes by and no one has given them any recognition, they're going to start running on fumes and not feel appreciated. By the time you finally do get around to it, it may not feel sincere. A lack of appreciation is one of the main reasons people leave their employers.

Also, don't let little things turn into bigger frustrations due to a failure to address them early. Instead, you should address the little things as you go about each day to develop your team. This is called coaching. It doesn't mean all these problems will go away and that you'll never have to have a tough conversation with an employee. Just make sure that they aren't surprised when you bring them to the office to chat about an issue.

They should have been told several times and know that they haven't been changing prior to that conversation. It will make that conversation a lot more productive and less defensive, because you aren't surprising them with news about their poor performance. It's not fair to your people to blind side them with critical feedback, and you wouldn't appreciate it if it happened to you.

Progress may seem like it's taking longer than you'd like. The first year in a new role can often make you feel disappointed if you didn't achieve your expectations. However, it's helpful to know that many people feel surprised at how far they've come when they look back on the prior five years or more. God's timing is always a factor.

Achieving Results

We aren't paid for how hard we work. We're paid when we generate the desired results that add value to others. You could work extremely hard and not get anywhere. Working hard is important, but you also need to work smart. If you don't, your month will fly by and you won't be as close to your goal as you had hoped. The best way to do this is to focus on the things that matter the most, and eliminate the things that are getting in the way. You need to channel both your energy and your team's energy into the things that achieve the desired results. You do this by looking at your current state, deciding on your goal state, identifying gaps, driving change, and managing performance.

Big Idea:

Engage in faithful activities, and trust God to provide the results.

CH 18 | Money

24 "No one can serve two masters. For you will hate one and love the other; you will be devoted to one and despise the other. You cannot serve God and be enslaved to money.

- Matthew 6:24 NLT

Managing Finances

Our businesses generate money. The way you manage money reveals what you really love. We all have to work to meet our needs, and almost everyone works to earn money. Money is our medium for trade in society. There have been different economic models that countries have used to manage their finances. For the most part, the United States is a capitalist society that believes in private property. Private businesses decide how goods are produced and the market decides how they are consumed. If you believe God has called you to start a business, then be thankful that we have the freedom to do that in the USA. We all have to manage our finances regardless of whether we're a business owner, a manager, or an employee.

We know that God owns everything, and we simply get to manage it while we're on Earth. We don't know how many years we'll be here or how much we'll be entrusted to manage while we're here. We just know that we need to be faithful stewards of every resource we have. The Christian business leader must put greed to death. We must put pride, envy, gluttony, and laziness to death with it. Regardless of the strategies you use, managing your finances well as a Christian is mostly a heart issue.

Financial Projections

In order to be profitable, you'll need a goal that is set at a number that enables you to become profitable. If you aim too low, your revenue may not be enough to cover your expenses and the business will fail. This is where you will need to use your Profit & Loss Statement. There are a few different financial projections you'll need to set. The first is your total revenue goal. It's helpful for businesses to think of this in terms of a percent of growth. On a P & L, a lot of businesses set their overall profit margin targets somewhere between 15-25%. If you add this margin to the total of all your expenses, you'll have your revenue target.

Another way to do this is to set it as a percentage of growth over the previous year assuming your expenses stay about the same. If you believe you can grow your total revenue by 5%, then that becomes your revenue target. There is a lot of financial and economic analysis that can be done to create a good forecast, and this is extremely important for large businesses who rely on external sources of capital.

For the small business owners, you may not be able to afford this type of research. You will often be making forecasts by looking at your business trends or changes you've made to the business. Lastly, every salesperson should have a sales target, and this is usually based on your past performance as well as your growth aspirations.

Expense Budget

Based on your financial projections, you'll need to determine your expense budget. This information is found on the bottom half of your P & L. This is where you decide in advance how you will spend the money in your business. What do you expect to spend to generate the revenues? How can you minimize some of these expenses?

One of the easiest areas to reduce expenses are to improve your inventory control processes. This is a source of problems that include waste, tied up capital, theft, loss from damage, and other things like this that raise your costs. Another way to reduce your expenses are to invest in more effective marketing strategies. Marketing is expensive, and it can be a source of wasted money when it's done poorly. There is a certain level of expected risk we need to understand about investing in marketing, but you should do your due diligence in making sure you're investing in the right places with the best tactics. You'll need to stop spending money on things that simply aren't working for you. Look for strategies that provide the best return on investment (ROI).

You can also set a goal to improve your profit margins. One of the keys to this are running more effective promotions that generate traffic without pricing all your products too low. Another aspect to this is setting realistic prices for things. If your cost of goods sold expense is increasing due to rising market prices, then you will usually have to raise your prices in order to protect your margins. It sounds obvious, but many businesses end up cutting in other places like labor out of fear that sales will be affected. One way a service business could look at this is that as the demand for your services increase, you can raise the fees to improve your margins. Demand often increases as your services improve. When more people want what you offer, you can usually raise prices a bit.

Ultimately, anything that can be measured or tracked in dollars should have a financial projection for it. You need to determine which ones are the most vital to your business in terms of tracking. You'll need to manage every line item on your P & L, but there are a few line items that have more impact on your profitability than others. You need to know what these are and monitor them closely.

Balanced Goals

For every financial projection you set, you need to count the cost. What will it really take to accomplish what you're hoping to achieve? The common temptation is to cut labor, because it's the easiest to do. The caution here is that it's extremely foolish to expect loyalty from your employees when you don't take care of them. In the real world, they end up in some level of rebellion that looks like mediocre service or even full blown protests. This is one of the reasons so many people in our country have started to question if capitalism produces the greatest good. I still fully believe in capitalism, but I am sensitive to why some people are so skeptical. There have been several cases of abuse. Regardless, when the employees hate working for a business and the public sees this, it has a direct impact on how the customers start to feel about the business, too. In other words, your brand is negatively affected.

You should strive to make decisions that are best for all stakeholders whenever possible. The best way to create balanced financial goals is to make decisions that would honor God in each area of your business. Don't cut your labor expense at your employees' detriment just to make more money for yourself or shareholders. You should only be cutting labor out of necessity and not out of greed. It's worth planning for a more conservative profit margin knowing that your employees and customers are being treated well.

Which groups of stakeholders do you serve?

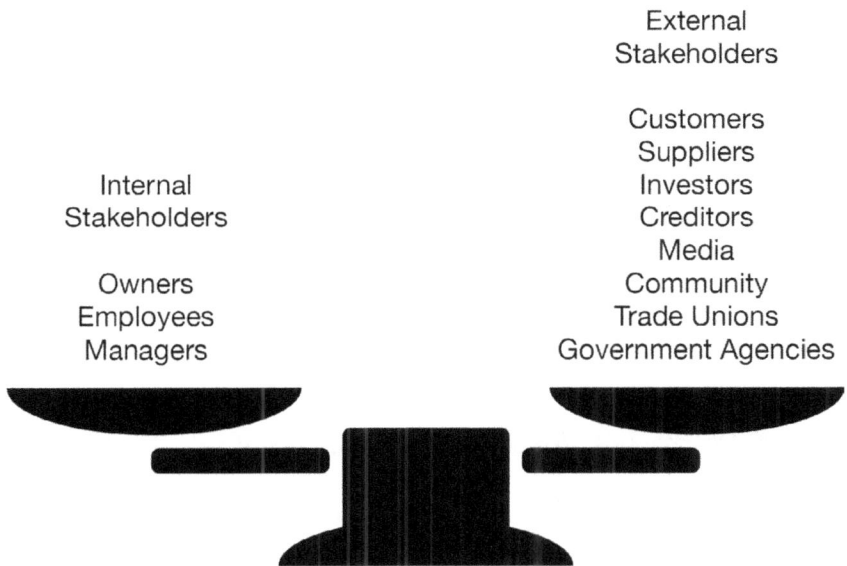

Internal
Stakeholders

Owners
Employees
Managers

External
Stakeholders

Customers
Suppliers
Investors
Creditors
Media
Community
Trade Unions
Government Agencies

Bigger Purpose

When God is our King and we are working for the Kingdom, profit isn't the primary concern that dictates all our decisions. Profit simply allows us to keep doing the mission. The mission provides the direction we need for our lives, and God provides the provision. One huge blessing you should consider as a Christian business leader is to donate a portion of your profits to the local church, a mission, or the community. God loves a cheerful giver, and businesses can be blessed by giving.

That's exactly what CEO David Green of Hobby Lobby does with the profits from his business. Each year, he and his team sit around a table and discern where God is asking them to invest in order to reach more people with the gospel. He is absolutely convinced that Hobby Lobby belongs to God, and He lets God decide what happens with the money.

Life is extremely short in light of eternity. Our days here are numbered, and we can't take any of our earthly wealth with us when we die. Only the treasures we store in heaven will last. Therefore, we have to stop looking at making money as a game to win. To become a Christian business leader, we need to stop serving two masters. Money is not the primary goal of our lives. Money is a wonderful gift, but the love of money is the root of all kinds of evil. Instead, we need to use our money as a tool to advance the Kingdom of God, and our businesses need to be managed well to generate profit. Seek to make every financial management decision with the bigger purpose of your life in mind.

Big Idea:

Manage money well to bless your employees and advance the Kingdom.

Part 2 | Build the Framework

Business Model | Good leaders understand how their business works.

Goals | God wants you to set goals, but He owns the outcomes.

Leadership | Being a leader is a great responsibility.

Management | Managing a business requires diligence.

Schedule | The right schedule includes your work, personal life, and rest.

Execution | The best results come when everyone is united around the company mission.

Results | Engage in faithful activities, and trust God to provide the results.

Money | Manage money well to bless your employees and advance the Kingdom.

Part 3 | Build the Business

	IMPACT
	CUSTOMER EXPERIENCE / CUSTOMER BASE
PART 3: BUILD THE BUSINESS	CUSTOMER JOURNEY
	INBOUND STRATEGY / OUTBOUND STRATEGY
	BRANDING

	RESULTS / MONEY
	SCHEDULE / EXECUTION
PART 2: BUILD THE FRAMEWORK	LEADERSHIP / MANAGEMENT
	GOALS
	BUSINESS MODEL

	LOVE
	WORK / GENEROSITY
PART 1: BUILD THE FOUNDATION	GIFTS / PROBLEMS / SERVICE
	MISSION / CALLING / MINISTRY
	GOD

CH 19 | Branding

10 For we are God's masterpiece. He has created us anew in Christ Jesus, so we can do the good things he planned for us long ago.

- Ephesians 2:10 NLT

Now that we've made it to Part 3, we are going to start talking about how to build the business you're in. Part 2 helped you analyze what makes it work. Part 3 is going to discuss what makes it grow. While Part 2 leans more towards the logical side of the brain, Part 3 will start to exercise your creative side. For me, I have always loved this part of business! Let's go!

Brand Masterpiece

A masterpiece demonstrates a high level of creativity and applied knowledge. It represents an example of an artist's greatest work. An artist may create several thousand pieces in their lifetime, but they are not all considered to be a masterpiece. A masterpiece may take an artist over a year to complete. There is a lot of thought, inspiration, effort, training, attention to detail, and passion that gets put into it. The Bible tells us that humans are God's masterpiece, and that He had both planned for us and designed us to do good things in this world.

God has created billions of individuals who either lived in the past, are living now, or are yet to be born. Each one of these people are one-of-a-kind. God puts great care and thought into our design, and every person has a unique purpose. The good things he planned for us to do are a part of our purpose. Therefore, if we are called to business, we will be doing good things through our businesses to serve others.

Christian entrepreneurs are given the responsibility to take a God-given idea and bring it to life. This created business will have some sort of a brand. A brand can be thought of in terms of how a customer feels about a business. There are a lot of tangible and intangible expressions of a brand. A brand is not just a logo. As the entrepreneur, you can influence the brand with your decisions, but the customers are the ones who experience the brand and define it.

The word "Christian" can be thought of as a brand. Jesus's followers never intended to call themselves Christians. They were simply people of "the way". Some of the Romans and Jews mocked them for their faith calling them "little Christs". In some ways, this was like their brand. They decided to run with it and adopted the label we know and use today calling themselves Christians.

Your experience of a brand is formed by every interaction you have with the business, including how it looks, who you interact with, your enjoyment of the product, what you hear, and a myriad of other things. These things all work together to establish the brand in your mind. All the work that goes into bringing this brand experience to life is the team's masterpiece. To build your brand masterpiece, it will take time, investment, care, creativity, and hard work.

Brand Brief

This is where it all begins. A brand brief is a summary of the major elements that help express a brand. A lot of work goes into the development of a brand brief, but having this document is helpful for guiding future decisions related to protecting the brand. The main idea in a brand brief is your brand essence, and all the elements of your brand should point to and support your brand essence. A brand essence is the explanation of your entire brand distilled down into a simple phrase.

The elements included in a brand brief will cover your

mission, vision, value propositions, key competitors, attributes, competitive advantage, target market, key stakeholders, key products and services, and anything else that helps explain your brand.

Purpose. The mission and vision of the business is where your purpose is explained. Each successful business solves an unmet need in the market in a way that customers desire. If it didn't, then the business wouldn't succeed. Why does your brand exist?

Position. There should be one thing that your target customer can get from you that they can't get anywhere else. If there isn't one, you will probably have a tough time keeping customers. You need to understand who is included in your target market and how you meet their needs differently than your competitors do. You should make a list of the key competitors in your geographic area and understand what they offer. Understanding your competitors allows you to discover your competitive advantage. This competitive advantage is one of the most important things you need to communicate through your promotional efforts.

Promise. The value propositions of your products and services tend to shape your brand promise. Delivering on your brand promise drives customer satisfaction. Satisfied customers often become repeat customers and tell their friends. What is your brand promise? Knowing the answer to that question can help you come up with a tagline or slogan for your brand.

The other thing you should think about is who you're making this promise to. You need to know who your key stakeholders are. One of these groups are your customers, but there are additional stakeholders that businesses usually serve. Common groups of stakeholders are your employees, suppliers, government, shareholders, and society at large. Your brand promise will connect with different stakeholders in different ways. You should get familiar with all the different stakeholders your business serves.

Personality. If your brand were a person, what would they be like? These features are called brand attributes. When someone experiences your brand, what does it look like, sound like, feel like, smell like, and/or taste like? How does your brand make them feel? What values are expressed? These types of qualities make it possible for a person to have a relationship with a brand. They may not know anyone who works at the business personally, but they may become customers simply from their interactions with the brand touchpoints. This is very common with online businesses. All of the elements that interact with a person's senses, mind, and heart help shape the personality of a brand.

Packaging. Packaging appeals to your customers' senses. Your key products and services shape how the customers think about your brand. Packaging is part of the product, and it helps customers make a decision about what to buy when faced with multiple options. Your brand packaging helps communicate your brand story and deserves a lot of consideration. For many products, if you set them side by side without packaging, they would look very similar. In some cases, they are the exact same thing. Corn is corn. The packaging attaches your brand's promises to the product.

Example of a Brand Brief

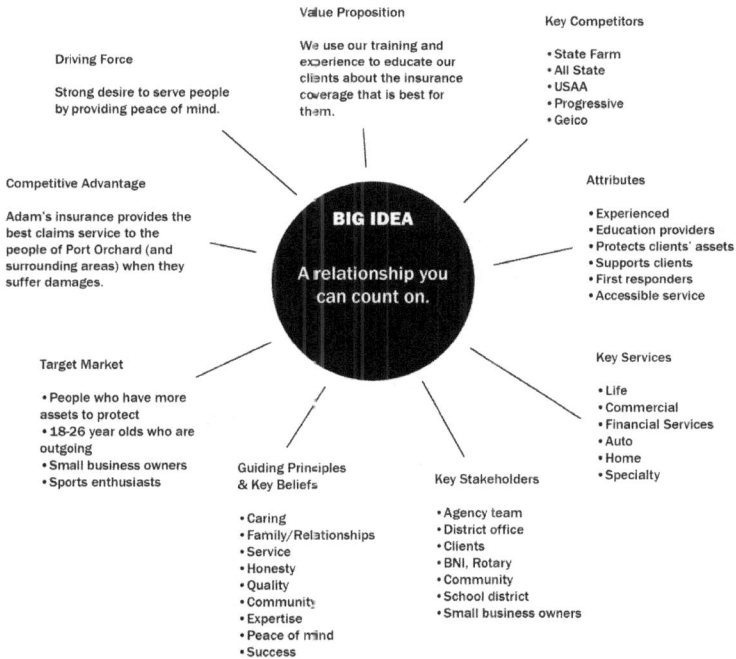

Value Proposition

We use our training and experience to educate our clients about the insurance coverage that is best for them.

Key Competitors

- State Farm
- All State
- USAA
- Progressive
- Geico

Driving Force

Strong desire to serve people by providing peace of mind.

Competitive Advantage

Adam's insurance provides the best claims service to the people of Port Orchard (and surrounding areas) when they suffer damages.

BIG IDEA

A relationship you can count on.

Attributes

- Experienced
- Education providers
- Protects clients' assets
- Supports clients
- First responders
- Accessible service

Target Market

- People who have more assets to protect
- 18-26 year olds who are outgoing
- Small business owners
- Sports enthusiasts

Key Services

- Life
- Commercial
- Financial Services
- Auto
- Home
- Specialty

Guiding Principles & Key Beliefs

- Caring
- Family/Relationships
- Service
- Honesty
- Quality
- Community
- Expertise
- Peace of mind
- Success

Key Stakeholders

- Agency team
- District office
- Clients
- BNI, Rotary
- Community
- School district
- Small business owners

Creating Your Brand Identity

Logo. Some businesses can succeed without a logo while others should consider investing in professional logo design. A logo helps you stand out from the competition and be remembered. The failure rate of businesses is very high, and it can seem risky to invest a lot of money in a logo. However, in some situations there's also a lot of risk in skimping on this part of your brand. A logo is used on a lot of different things that customers see. Its primary job is to help customers pick your brand out of a crowd. Is your current logo helping your business or hindering it?

Typography. The style of typefaces you choose will communicate just as much about your brand as your graphics and photos do. Each typeface that is well known was designed for a specific purpose. The biggest problem I see with some businesses is that they never took the time to decide which typefaces would represent their brand, and this causes them to use far too many. They are chosen at random, and every new typeface that is used dilutes the clarity of the brand identity. Haphazardly selected typefaces will give off an unintended brand message. Lastly, you need to figure out how you want to express the different elements of your copy including headlines, quotations, body, citations, and any other printed communication.

Color Palette. A consistent use of color is another important aspect of visual identity systems. Your core brand collateral will need a consistent palette in order to be remembered. When you think about your favorite brands, you can usually state the one or two dominant colors of the brand. If I ask you to think of companies where blue is the dominant color, who do you think of first? How about green or red? Which holiday do you think of when you see green and red together? I hope you can see that your answers to those questions were once a decision a designer had to make. What colors differentiate your brand from your competition?

Style. You'll need to decide on a style of the graphics and photos you will use. The styles can change over time, but it's extremely helpful to use graphics or photos that all have a similar style as part of your brand identity system. These assets work together with your logo, typefaces, and colors to create your design aesthetic. Some common design styles include retro, luxury, geometric, minimalist, feminine, 3-D, abstract, typography focused, illustrative, playful, or grunge. In photography, you usually deal with things like genres, focus, saturation, composition, artistic expression, and editing styles. The style alone communicates far more than you may realize, so it's important to choose the style that represents your brand the best.

Messaging. The last thing I'll mention as it relates to your brand identity is messaging. This is the voice of your brand. It includes elements like your company name, taglines or slogans, mission and vision statements, key messages, boilerplate, elevator pitch, and any company lingo that you use regularly. The way a company writes and communicates reflects their brand personality and values. This is one of the reasons for having people on your team who are responsible for communications. The way your brand communicates causes your customers to feel a certain way about the brand and what it represents. Take the time to make sure you are communicating the right messages.

Bringing It Together

As you think through these different elements of your brand, I hope you can see how they all work together to help influence your customers' brand experience. Building a strong brand is an important step in creating a thriving business. Every time a customer interacts with one of your brand's touchpoints, a perception is formed. Investing the proper amount of effort, creativity, and resources into building your brand will almost always give you a return far greater than that which you put in.

Big Idea:

Treat your brand identity like it's a masterpiece.

CH 20 | Customer Journey

4 On the third day of their journey, Abraham looked up and saw the place in the distance.

- Genesis 22:4 NLT

Every Interaction Counts

A customer journey turns strangers into fans, and the touchpoints working together at different stages help the person get to that point. Marketers analyze the customer journey to map out all of the places customers have interactions with a brand. You don't always get to interact with every customer in person. However, your customers will experience your brand through every encounter with your business whether they be your print ads, online presence, store, radio ads, sales team, or some other fashion. You will have control over some of these activities, and you may have no direct control over others like PR or Word of Mouth. Nevertheless, every interaction a prospect or customer has with your brand either causes them to move towards becoming a satisfied customer or checking out your competition.

The cost of acquiring a customer is an important consideration for any business. The marketing you are doing will either help you build or break these customer relationships. The moment you run out of customers is the moment you are out of business. That's why every interaction counts. No business can stay open long term if they aren't helping people move through the customer journey stages. The business will eventually fail from lack of revenue.

Ideally, each promotional activity your business uses should help guide the prospect towards becoming a highly satisfied customer. There are different stages the customer goes through, and there are different interactions they will need at each stage. It's your responsibility to make sure those things are placed exactly where your prospects and customers can easily find them.

Stages

If you do an Internet search for customer journey, then you will notice that marketers call each stage something a little different as well as have a different number of recognized stages. As a general rule, they are all fairly similar in their purpose. The differences between how marketers explain a customer journey are subtle most of the time. Choose the one that makes the most sense to you and your context. Here is one way to look at the different stages:

Awareness - a person goes from having never heard about your brand to discovering it for the first time. It is the first impression they have with your brand. It usually takes seeing it a few times before they actually *see* it. If your brand captures their attention as a potential solution to whatever need or want they have, they will usually move to the next stage.

Consideration - This is where they start to learn more about what you have to offer. They are exploring their options and kicking some tires. Once they begin to believe that you may have what they want, they start moving towards making a decision.

Decision - They are deeper in your sales process at this point. There are a lot of reasons why they might be interested in your product. They need to make sure it's really what they want before they commit, so help them get all the information they need to make a decision.

Service - After they buy your product or service, you must deliver on your promises. The experience they have with your brand at this point is critical. Will they be pleased with their purchase, or will they have buyer's remorse? Your job is to help them have confidence that doing business with your brand was a great decision. If you do that well, the customer usually moves into the final stage.

Advocacy - This is the stage you should try to help every customer want to get to, because this is where they tell their friends and come back for more. This is where businesses really experience growth. This is where word of mouth moves your next prospect into the Awareness stage, and the customer journey for that new prospect begins.

Touchpoints

A touchpoint is each and every interaction a prospect or customer has with your brand. Some of these touchpoints come in the form of inbound and outbound marketing. Inbound marketing involves activities that pull prospects towards you while outbound marketing involves activities that push your message out to prospects. Having the right touchpoint in the right place at the right time is incredibly important to maximize sales.

What do you Have?

On page 161, I gave you some space to think about your Customer Journey Map. As you think about the promotional activities that your business invests in, which stage does each activity fit into? Do you write a blog? Do you send out direct mail? Do you have salespeople? Do you run radio ads? What is the goal of each of your promotional activities?
After you have filled out your map, what initial thoughts do you have? What does this reveal to you about the strengths and opportunities of your current customer

journey? Taking an inventory of these activities and placing them on this map gives you a high-level view of what your prospects and customers are actually experiencing when they interact with your brand. You probably have a good idea of the ones that seem to help your business more than others. Take a moment to circle the top one or two promotional activities in each stage that you believe contribute the most to helping people move through this customer journey.

What do you Need?

Are any of the things on your map a waste of your resources? Every business has a marketing budget, and most people know they should be trying to maximize their return on investment in these areas. You may have tried something that isn't helping your business as much as you had hoped, and this means that you have an opportunity cost to consider. Doing this ineffective promotional activity is actually preventing you from using those same resources in a more productive manner. You should consider eliminating the activities that provide little to no value and redeploy those resources in a more productive area.

Next, try and find the bottlenecks in your process. Where are customers getting stuck on the journey? From my experience, most businesses struggle in the very first stage by not capturing enough awareness for their brand. You may have a different challenge. In which stage are people no longer moving forward as frequently as you'd like? Is there a promotional activity that is missing from your mix?

Having a well-planned and executed customer journey is a game changer for a business. Most businesses cannot afford to do a lot of different things due to their limited resources, but you should have at least one effective touchpoint in each stage that helps turn strangers into fans. Based on the high rate of failure, I wouldn't consider this exercise "optional". If you want people to become advocates of your brand and bring their friends, you have to look at your process and make the necessary changes to help them get to that stage.

Customer Journey Map

Awareness >>> Consideration >>> Decision >>> Service >>> Advocacy

Stage	What do we have now?	What do we need to add?
Awareness		
Consideration		
Decision		
Service		
Advocacy		

Big Idea:

Help people get where they want to go.

CH 21 | Inbound Strategy

8 Give thanks to the Lord and proclaim his greatness.
Let the whole world know what he has done.

- 1 Chronicles 16:8 NLT

Promotion

In marketing, promotion is one of the traditional "4 P's"; Product, Price, Place, and Promotion. The goal of promotion is to get the word out in the market about what you're selling. The marketing communication strategies you use can create awareness, interest, sales, and brand loyalty.

Today, most marketers use a combination of inbound and outbound strategies. Inbound pulls prospects towards your brand so that they initiate contact. Outbound pushes your messages out, and you are the one driving the contact. There are tremendous benefits to inbound marketing. It's affordable, it isn't pushy, it builds up over time, and it tends to be shared taking your messages even farther. It is more accessible to small businesses than traditional promotional marketing, because it really only takes a few tools, time, and talent to produce.

Inbound marketing seeks to create valuable content that people are searching for. The building blocks of content include text, pictures, sounds, and video. Content tends to either be entertaining or educational, but sometimes it's both. Inbound marketing can be used in many different ways. I've listed a few of them on the following chart.

Websites	Media	People	Social Media
- Blogging	- Press releases	- Influencers	- Viral marketing
- Email	- Newsroom	- Public speaking	- Video content
- Feedback	- Exclusives	- Word of mouth	- Infographics
- Search Engine Optimization (SEO)		- Podcasting	- Brand images
- Pay-Per-Click (PPC)		- Meetings	- Ads
- Knowledge base		- Calling	- Likes and subscribes
- Live chat		- Events	
- Bots			
- Marketing automation			
- Inbound links			
- Analytics			

Digital Channels

Paid - an example is social media ads like on Facebook, Instagram, LinkedIn, and Twitter.

Earned - where individuals and other sites want to share your content.

Owned - these are the digital channels you have control over like your own social pages, website, and blog.

Inbound Marketing

You'll need to figure out which strategies compliment your brand the best. You'll also need to create some content. What do you create? You create things that add value to your audience that they're already searching for. That's why you need to understand the needs of your audience. Again, they usually want to be entertained, educated, or both. To help you understand this, just visit the social media channel of a brand you like and pay attention to what they show you. What does their content communicate? A video of someone surfing is usually entertaining, but if they are teaching you how to surf, then it's educational (or maybe both). Now think about your brand. What can you share with the world that they would find interesting enough to give you their attention?

Creating content isn't easy, and it can be very time consuming. One really smart way to get more out of your content creation is to multi-purpose it. If you create a long-form piece of content like a white paper or book, you can always pull out components of it to be used in other ways. You can pull out quotes, find images that communicate the same message, design an infographic, do a podcast on that topic, post it in your F.A.Q.s, give a live talk, create a webinar, and many other things.

The content you create will be based on the marketing communications strategy for your business. You need to decide what it is, which channel it will be on, and when you want to share your content. You'll put this strategy on a calendar. Marketing communication is just as much an art as it is a science. It takes testing and adjusting. The challenge to inbound is that so many other companies are finally starting to do it, so you have tons of competition for people's attention. However, the benefits outweigh the cost, and you'll want to figure out how to use inbound strategies to your company's advantage.

Budget

Recommended marketing budgets tend to be about 5% of gross revenue for a company. Yours may be a little more or a little less. Regardless of how much money you have, you'll need to know how much money you have to work with and make decisions on where to spend those dollars. You don't need to advertise in the highest number of places to be effective. It might help, but you really just need to be in the most productive places. Focus the bulk of your budget on the things that bring the most attention, and don't worry about the rest.

Evaluating Effectiveness

These strategies do cost time and money even though inbound marketing is typically cheaper than outbound efforts. Most of these web-based strategies have reporting available for them. You can take a look at what you're spending and how well it's working. You may be tempted at times to give up on using a particular medium if you aren't seeing results, but you need to know that it usually isn't the medium's fault.

You could be using the right medium in the wrong way, and you'll need to fix the content. Don't abandon the strategy too soon. It isn't easy to figure out how to get people's attention, because there is a lot more competition for their attention than ever before. The best thing you can do is to make a decision where you're going to try and get attention and fully commit for at least one year. Get advice or help when needed, and don't give up. The more you can tell your brand story, the better chance you'll have that your customers will find you.

CREATE VALUABLE CONTENT

Big Idea:

Create valuable content for people, and they will find you.

CH 22 | Outbound Strategy

3 Never let loyalty and kindness leave you!
   Tie them around your neck as a reminder.
   Write them deep within your heart.

4 Then you will find favor with both God and people,
   and you will earn a good reputation.

- Proverbs 3:3-4 NLT

Outbound Marketing

Outbound strategies are what traditional marketers have relied on for centuries to get a message out to the public about a product, service, event, opportunity, or idea. These messages are sent through television, radio, direct mail, cold calling, sales, billboards, trade shows, and many other forms. These traditional forms still work, but they tend to be expensive. Advertising and selling are two outbound strategies that nearly every business still needs to do along with their inbound strategies.

Advertising

Advertising is about sending messages out quickly and at scale at a relatively low cost per person. These messages are called advertisements. The goal of advertising is getting as much reach as possible with the people most likely to want what you have so you can generate new business. The type of advertising medium you decide on should give you the best opportunity to do this. While you are working on drawing in new customers through inbound marketing, you should also send messages out. You need to figure out what medium your specific audience is paying attention to. Facebook ads might work for one demographic; magazine ads might work for another.

You can create your own ads or work with an agency. Most small businesses do not have the budget to be able to use an agency or the more expensive mediums. This is why social media ads are so popular for small business owners. The attention is relatively cheap, and the ability to define and target specific audiences is unmatched. You also get reporting data that helps you understand the effectiveness of your ad. Keep in mind that most ads will need to be seen multiple times before a prospect actually *sees* it. We're bombarded with messages every day, and only a few of them are actually grabbing our attention. Most ads do best with repetition.

Purposes of an Advertisement

Here are a few common reasons why you would advertise:

- to inform consumers about your product or service
- to stimulate demand
- to explain the benefits of using your product
- to help consumers decide which commodity to choose
- to build confidence or reduce doubt and confusion
- to persuade people to take action now
- to raise awareness and goodwill for your organization

To create an effective ad, you need to decide on what you're trying to get a consumer to do. Once you know what your goal is, you can begin to decide how you're going to influence them to do it.

Elements of an Advertisement

Copy & Text - the words you use need to be clear, brief, and to the point. Copy usually includes at least a headline that grabs the person's attention and some body text that sells the message. A lot of companies will include their slogan. The reason most ads have to be brief is that you typically only have a few seconds to communicate before you lose their attention.

Photos, Graphics, & Illustrations - these images are usually what is noticed first in an ad, and they must work together with your copy to communicate your message. This also includes your company logo. You need to make decisions as to whether or not to go with color or black and white depending on where the ad will be placed.

Layout - graphic designers understand that layout affects the way a viewer reads your ad. Good layouts will help people notice the most important elements of your ad and in the right order. In the west, we read from left to right and top to bottom. Ads in the west usually follow this layout for this reason. The size and space dedicated to each element assists with this.

Placement - where will the ad be placed and on which medium? Is it a still image, video commercial, or radio-style ad? Is it print or digital? These decisions will affect the kind of options you have and how much space or time you have to work with. The best ads are placed where the most interested audience will receive them. Each medium has a different cost and reach. You'll need to figure out where your ads will create the best return on investment based on the purpose of the ad.

Personal Selling

Advertising can reach a large audience much faster than selling, but it is less effective per person. Selling is slower since you're usually speaking to one customer at a time, but you get the chance to tailor your communication to each person. While your advertisements are working to reach as many people as possible in your target market, you or your team should be engaged in personal selling activities.

Everyone sells something. The higher priced or more complicated products like a house or automobile usually have longer sales processes, while simpler products like clothing or food have much shorter ones. Personal selling involves direct communication between a seller and a buyer. The seller communicates information and uses persuasion to encourage a prospect to buy. Good salespeople seek out and stimulate new sales opportunities for their organizations.

Relationships with Customers

The goal of trade is to create an exchange of value. Most products will need to be purchased multiple times, because they are consumable or wear out with use. The best companies do a good job building long-term relationships with their customers by consistently providing value. A good relationship will encourage the buyer to go back to the same seller over and over. These sales cycles might happen daily or every few years based on the thing you sell. Taking great care of your customers so you can retain them is the real key to growing any business.

Networking & Prospecting

Everyone who has to use personal selling in their business should focus on networking first. Networking is simply building new relationships. You introduce yourself to others and get to know a little about them. As you build your network, you will need to start prospecting. Prospecting is the first step in the sales process where you are trying to figure out who in your network might need your product or service. These are called leads. Sometimes leads come to you, but most of the time you'll need to seek after them.

If you have 1000 people in your network, then you could think about each person's needs and come up with a list of leads. As you communicate with each lead, you will find out whether or not they have a real need and ability to buy. If they do, that's when they become prospects. The next step where you ask questions and do a needs assessment is called qualification.

Making it Easy

Prospecting is one of the things that is hardest for most salespeople. Most salespeople secretly hope a qualified prospect will walk through the door, tell them exactly what they need, and allow them to skip right into the presentation. These salespeople tend to wait around a lot, because they aren't using their time wisely by prospecting for new business. The most common reason for this is they have not yet learned the easy way to do it.

The best way to do this is to be kind and loyal to everyone you meet. This is the secret to networking. Most salespeople know they should be networking, but they feel awkward or intimidated. The truth is that it's easier than you think. Just hang out where people are who are likely to want what you sell. You don't have to impress anyone or know a lot of funny jokes. Kindness and loyalty is enough. If you will simply let enough people know what you do and where you work, you will be amazed at what happens. People will usually volunteer some kind of information to let you know whether or not they are interested in what you sell. If they seem extremely interested, resist the urge to launch into a presentation on the spot. It isn't the right time. Instead, get some kind of contact information from them and follow up later. This is a great way to build a list of leads.

The other easy way to build a list of leads is to start with all the people you already know, let them know what you're selling, and come up with a question that enables you to learn whether or not they have a need. The best questions feel natural and have no pressure. If you find out they do have a need, the next step is to try and figure out how urgent that need is. People who want to solve something now will usually set an appointment with you to learn more. If they don't need to solve it for awhile, then you will put them into your follow up system and try again later.

One thing to keep in mind here is that you can often increase their interest the same way ads do. Ways to increase a sense of urgency are things like limited-time offers or limited-inventory. They may realize that even though they weren't planning on doing anything now, the deal is just too good to pass up. Prospecting skills boil down to simply meeting more people, understanding their needs, and staying in touch. The more you do this, the easier it will be to find qualified prospects.

Using Today's Tools

It wasn't that long ago where all these sales efforts were done using paper or index cards. Today, we have some amazing tools at our disposal that make all this work easier. One tool every sales organization needs is a Customer Relationship Management (CRM) program. These programs are a type of database that store information about your leads and notes about the contacts you make with them.

Another amazing tool that we have at our disposal is social media. Early sales efforts focused on getting contact information, trying to gather and record bits of information about who people are, and maintaining relationships. Today, people do that work for you on their own social media profiles! Not only do they tell you a lot about them, they also keep all the information updated in real time.

Lastly, smart phones are amazing! My first cell phone had one function; it called people without being attached to a wall. Today, smart phones provide us with all the sales tools we could possibly ask for at our fingertips through various apps. This allows us to be more productive, build relationships faster, and communicate with them in many different ways. This makes selling easier than ever before for people who understand how to sell.

Having the Right Attitude

You're either going to push your product or service into the market for selfish reasons with a winner take all attitude, or you're going to do it because you really believe it helps people. You're either going to use people to get money, or you're going to see them as people to love and serve. As Christians, we are called to have the mind of Christ.

We need to be very careful in how we view advertising and selling. Also, we need to be careful to not view ourselves as the source of our own income. We plant seeds, we water them, but God makes them grow. This applies to winning people for Christ as well as growing an organization. Every human being we come into contact with is loved by God and made in His image. We must make every effort to do our jobs with the right attitude towards others and treat them with the respect they deserve.

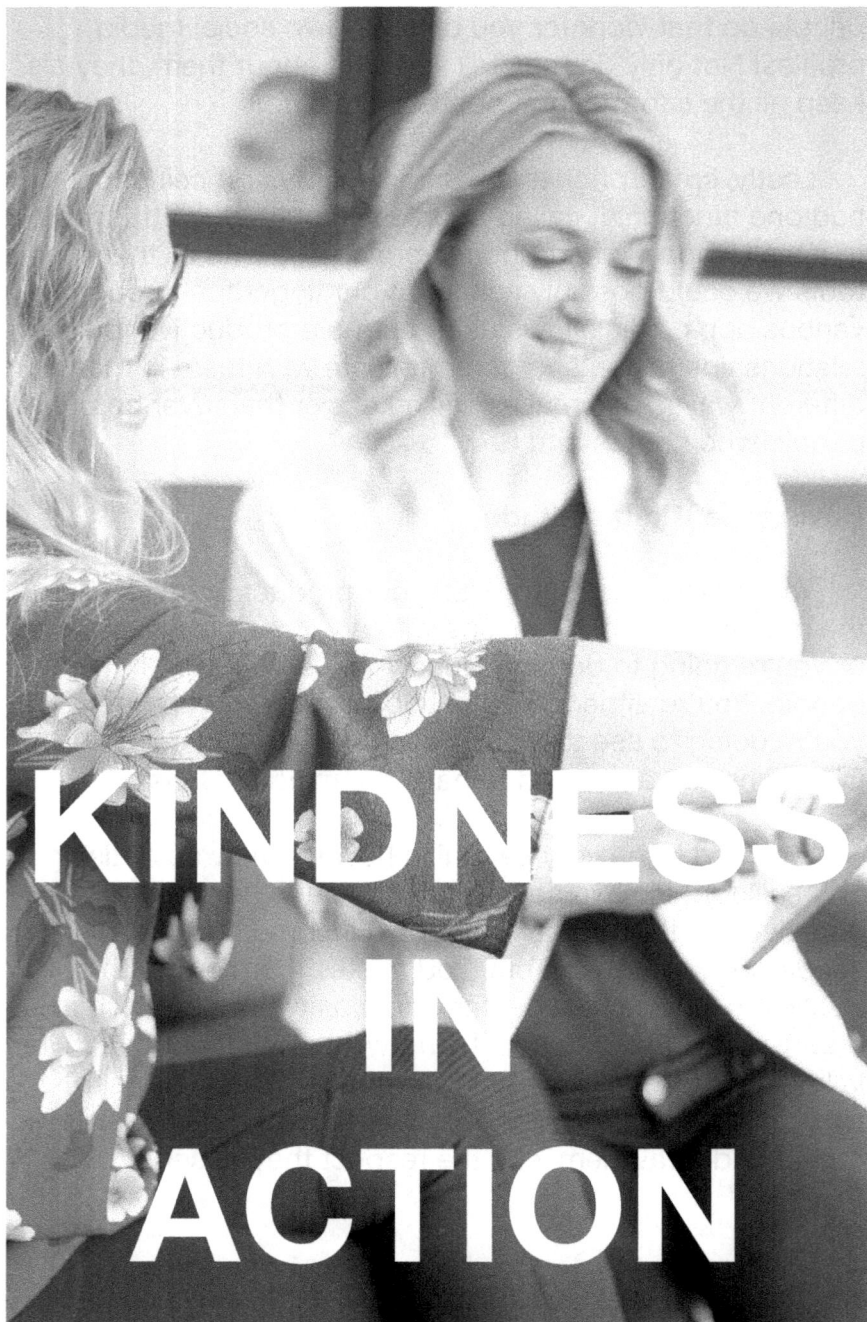

KINDNESS IN ACTION

Big Idea:

Finding customers starts with being kind and loyal to everyone you meet.

CH 23 | Customer Experience

30 The seeds of good deeds become a tree of life;
   a wise person wins friends.

- Proverbs 11:30 NLT

Handcrafting Experiences

After your inbound and outbound marketing strategies have been at work, you should start to have prospects show up. The first experience they have with your business is incredibly important. First, you want to make sure you do a great job serving them. You exchange products and services with these people for your income, so you better treat them right. Also, if they do have a great experience, then they will probably do business with you again in the future and refer their friends.

The best businesses examine every part of the customer experience from the customer's perspective. The experience starts in the parking lot. These first impressions are important. Next, they will walk through your door. What do they experience in the first 60 seconds? Every business is different as to what happens next, but the customer experience usually ends with some sort of transaction. After the transaction is completed, you still might not be done. What activities need to happen after they leave? Every moment of the customer experience should be well thought out and create high levels of satisfaction. Similar considerations are important even if your business is done 100% online.

There are lots of different ways products and services are delivered to customers. You'll need to think about how your business works and if there is anything you can do to improve the customer experience. You may have one of the best products in the world, but if the way they are purchased is frustrating to your customers, then it will be hard for your business to succeed. With access to more information and options, the public is far less tolerant than they used to be of a poor experience with a business.

Sales Process

Every product or service has a sales process, and they are all very similar. Low-priced products typically have a much faster process than high-ticket ones. Selling lemonade is obviously simpler than selling airplanes. Ultimately, the process your company uses is there for a reason. If you could sell an airplane as easy as a glass of lemonade, then you wouldn't need a different process. Factors like price, risk, complexity, fear, expectations, languages, negotiations, and other considerations naturally complicate a sales process. You need to understand what the best sales process is for your type of business and stick closely to it.

After the lead is qualified through asking great questions and becomes a prospect, what happens next? You will need to help select the product or service that you think is right for them and present it as a solution. Complicated products may also require a demonstration to help sell them. Doing a great job qualifying the lead, selecting a solution, presenting it, and demonstrating how it works will put you in position to make the sale.

Closing

Closing is asking a customer to buy, and it's often simpler than we make it. Every time you help a customer feel like your solution is the right one during the sales process, you are closing. The final closing question needs to be asked at the right time. You can try and close too soon, which is before you've built the value in owning it. You can also close too late (and even spoil a sale) by talking too much. When is the right time? You should try and close the sale once you have reasonable confidence that the prospect wants what you have.

There are a few easy ways to wrap up a sale rather than just saying, "Do you want to buy it?". You can simply assume the sale by asking how they would like to purchase it. If they offer a method of payment, then they've essentially said, "yes." Another way is you can make a suggestion connected to owning the product such as delivery times and then ask them if it works for them. A "yes" is also typically a confirmation of the sale. You can give them a few options where picking one is understood as agreement to buy. Lastly, you can use an event that creates a sense of urgency, like a promotion ending, to see if they want to take advantage of it now. There are lots of books available with closing techniques, but these four work for almost any industry.

My caution to you with some techniques is that there is an area you can move towards that is unethical manipulation, and I certainly don't believe this honors God or is loving to your neighbor. You'll need to follow your conscience in these matters. Also, you will almost always get some objections. Some are simpler than others, and not all objections can be overcome. If you can ethically satisfy these objections, then you definitely should. Your customers often need more information before they can make a good decision.

However, this is another area of caution when it comes to closing. You're often going to feel some temptation to do or say whatever it takes to close a sale out of pressure to earn money. As soon as you start getting into the area of half-truths, you've gone too far. It's better to let the customer leave and trust God to send another customer than to try and trick them into buying something.

When a customer says "no" for now, thank them for their time and move on. When they say "yes", you'll need to wrap up the transaction and deliver the product. Thank them for their business, and take care of any other needed activities.

Follow Up

After the customer has left, there are a lot of businesses that will need to follow up as part of their process to maintain the relationship or offer further service. This is an area of the sales process that is often neglected by salespeople. Take the time to do this well, and it will pay dividends. You've worked hard getting a customer to this point and invested a certain amount of money acquiring them. It's a really bad idea to lose them at this point by not investing a few additional minutes every once in awhile on follow up. Again, every business is different, and follow up activities vary. The basic goal of follow up is that you commit to keeping in touch and providing value. Excellent follow up is the secret to repeat and referral business, and these are the keys to building a satisfied customer base. This is the essence of good stewardship.

One Last Thought

If nothing else, think about it like this:

What kind of experience with you and your business do you want them to tell their friends and family about? The great one they had or the horrible one?

The answer to that question will help you know exactly what you should do to treat them well and ensure a great customer experience.

Big Idea:

Treating customers well helps turn strangers into friends.

CH 24 | Customer Base

6 Remember this—a farmer who plants only a few seeds will get a small crop. But the one who plants generously will get a generous crop.

- 2 Corinthians 9:6 NLT

Every Customer Counts

The difference between average businesses and exceptional ones is usually reflected in how well they serve customers. There are a lot of businesses that open for the day, go through the motions, help some people, and close up until tomorrow. These businesses seem to get by, but they never seem to grow. There are other businesses that understand how important each customer is and do an amazing job taking care of them. They steadily grow the customer base year over year, and the company expands its territory. They also seem to create ten times the results of the average companies.

Could it be that simple? Judge for yourself. Go into any business you want and see how well you are served. You will notice a correlation between their service and their success. The businesses that work hard to retain their customers usually do, and the ones who don't seem to care are always scrambling and spending money to find new ones. Constantly trying to acquire new customers is expensive, so it makes no sense to be negligent in the care of your customers.

The Secret to Growth

Planting more seeds gives you a much better chance of growing a generous crop. Serving more people gives you a better chance of increased sales. This Biblical principle works in ministry as well as business. However, you can only reach so many people yourself. Taking great care of your customers will cause some of them to expand your reach through no additional effort of your own. It has a multiplying effect that works far better than any advertising campaign you can think of. What does it take? You have to genuinely care about people.

A single seed can become a tree that bears thousands more seeds over time. That's one thing you can do with a seed. The other thing you can do with a seed is consume it, but you won't get the tree. This is the system God created, and it's brilliant.

Advocates

An advocate publicly supports a person or cause. Jesus is our advocate before the Father. If you love people and serve them well, many of them will become your advocates. As your business grows, your team must grow with it and maintain this passion for service. Your employees are one source of advocates. Growth makes customer satisfaction more difficult, but it isn't impossible. You simply need to focus on your company's culture and training system. This is what discipleship looks like in business. You train up leaders to carry out the mission.

Customers are your other source of advocates. You'll need a CRM system in businesses that must maintain individual relationships. Ideally, you would earn one advocate at a time, and you'd maintain that relationship as long as possible. You would grow from one to ten, ten to a hundred, a hundred to a thousand, and so on. You will need to decide how to do this at scale for your business. Typically, the more customers you have, the more employees you'll need. We all have a relational capacity, and when we exceed it the quality of the relationships suffer. The more you invest in both groups of people, the greater chance you'll have for multiplication.

The Vineyard

Jesus taught us in the book of John that He is the true vine, God the Father is the gardener, and we are the branches who will produce good fruit as long as we stay connected to the vine. While the context of this scripture wasn't intended for business, those of you who are called to business are still commanded to produce fruit. The business principles in this book are simple, but they work. Regardless of how big your business becomes, it needs to always remain focused on the fruit that will last. The money you earn will be quickly spent, but the impact you make can last an eternity. Stewardship should be your guiding force; not greed or haughtiness.

God lets us use His stuff for awhile, and we have to use it well. When we die, it won't matter how many dollars we had in the bank. God will hold us accountable for how we handled what He gave us. He'll talk to us about our customer interactions. He'll talk to us about how we treated our employees and coworkers. He'll talk to us about whether or not we neglected our families.

Vineyards can be vast, but they all have a point in which they stop. It's okay to have boundaries on your business where you realize you no longer need to expand to fulfill what God has planned for you. Work hard and invest in as many people as possible, but just know that God may call you to rest at some point. That realization is the balance to pursuing growth. Until you reach that point, work hard to take care of people and enjoy the blessings God gives you.

Healthy growth requires tender care.

Big Idea:

Big results often follow a big investment in people.

CH 25 | Impact

11 Yet God has made everything beautiful for its own time. He has planted eternity in the human heart, but even so, people cannot see the whole scope of God's work from beginning to end.

- Ecclesiastes 3:11 NLT

Keeping Things in Perspective

One of the biggest problems we share as human beings is that we often lack a proper perspective on time. Our thoughts are often focused on the moments we are in or somewhere in the past. We usually don't take much time to think about how brief our lives are compared to the scope of eternity. We also regularly fail to see what God is doing in and through our lives.

Our work is a gift. The skills, passions, and opportunities we have help us do our work. The work we do is important, but how much of it will actually last? The reality for every person on the planet is that we brought nothing into this world when we were born, and we can't take any of it with us when we die. The part of our work that we need to focus on the most is the part that is eternal. That part is the impact we make through our businesses to help all people have a relationship with Jesus. In our workplace, we may not be able to share Jesus with our words, but Jesus lives inside His believers. They're going to meet Jesus if we love people the way He loved them.

That is one of the major differences between just building a business and building a Christian business. Businesses are usually designed to generate short-term profits. Kingdom businesses are stewarded to promote eternal relationships. You are not alive just to accumulate stuff. Your report card on life is not tied to your net worth. Your title or salary are not a part of your identity. As you seek to build a Christian business, you must strive to keep these things in perspective. After all, the USA only began in 1776, and we're only living during a small part of it. No one knows what tomorrow holds except God. We must keep time in its proper perspective.

Everything Counts

You don't exist to merely serve yourself and meet your own needs. You serve the King of Kings and the Lord of Lords. All things were made through Him and for Him. The people, places, and circumstances you find yourself in are not accidents. And the things you do for our King are never wasted. Everything counts!

Most of us are not easily impressed these days, so we overlook the impact of the little things. We make comparisons about what we have or what we are doing in relation to others. When we look at our human heroes, we often think we could never do what they do. We really shouldn't envy them. Instead, we should simply celebrate how God made them.

We should also understand that we're not competing with them. We need to run our own race. Most of life is made up of a lot of little moments that seem insignificant at the time. However, they are usually far more impactful than we think. We know lots of stories about people who had one impactful encounter with someone else, and that encounter changed the entire course of their lives. Would you think about a short conversation differently if you knew it would change someone's life? How about their eternity? In God's hands, a few fish and loaves of bread fed over 5000 people. With God, nothing is ever insignificant, and nothing is ever wasted.

Well Done!

You are going to stand before God one day and give an account for your life. We all are. What are you going to say for yourself about how you spent the time He gave you? What do you want to hear from God? If you live your life selfishly and only for your own personal gain, then you may find yourself facing an angry God. Or, you can spend your life seeking after what is truly good and hear God say, "Well done!"

My prayer for every person who reads this book is that they would understand how much God loves them. I want you to have a successful business and be prosperous, but I really want you to understand that above all else, God wants a personal relationship with you. He wants you to love Him back and for you to love your neighbors. The business you steward is a vehicle to demonstrate His love to the world. If you made a list of all the people you know, how many of them do you want to receive eternal life? I hope you said, "All of them." That's the real impact you can be a part of through your business. You should lead the business with excellence and meet peoples' needs, but the biggest need we all have is Jesus.

I got into business with the sole purpose of pursuing money. I grew up poor, and all I wanted was to figure out how to get rich. Money was my god at the time. Then I met Jesus, and He showed me that my life was so much more important than money. In the United States of America, we cling to life, liberty, and the pursuit of happiness. You see celebrities chasing money and fame only to find out that it doesn't really make you happy. True happiness is only found in knowing our Lord and Savior, Jesus Christ. That's why Jesus came. It was His rescue mission, and He will return one day.

Proverbs 21:21 states, "Whoever pursues righteousness and love finds life, prosperity and honor." In Matthew 6:31-33, Jesus said, 31 "So don't worry about these things, saying, 'What will we eat? What will we drink? What will we wear?' 32 These things dominate the thoughts of unbelievers, but your heavenly Father already knows all your needs. 33 Seek the Kingdom of God above all else, and live righteously, and he will give you everything you need." You see, we don't need to try and pursue "things" to make us happy. It's a distortion of what I think the founding fathers of our country intended.

Instead, we need to pursue living life the way God tells us to and love others. He promises to take care of the rest. I challenge you to begin to lead your business from this perspective. I guarantee that even if your business remains small, you will make a huge impact on others through your life. And one day, God will reward you for it. One day, God will look you in the eyes with a great big heavenly smile and say, "Well done, good and faithful servant!"

Big Idea:

God takes the little we do and uses it for an eternal purpose.

Part 3 | Build the Business

Branding | Treat your brand identity like it's a masterpiece.

Customer Journey | Help people get where they want to go.

Inbound Strategy | Create valuable content for people, and they will find you.

Outbound Strategy | Finding customers starts with being kind and loyal to everyone you meet.

Customer Experience | Treating customers well helps turn strangers into friends.

Customer Base | Big results often follow a big investment in people.

Impact | God takes the little we do and uses it for an eternal purpose.

I wonder where God wil lead you...   200

Conclusion

13 If you are wise and understand God's ways, prove it by living an honorable life, doing good works with the humility that comes from wisdom.

- James 3:13 NLT

Congrats! You made it through the book. There's a lot to think about, isn't there? I felt the same way as I was trying to write it. The reality is that each one of these chapters could easily be its own book, but I trust you probably have access to books on many of these individual topics. The two big things I hope you take away from this book are an overview of your life as a Christian business leader as well as a couple of things you can put into practice immediately.

Keep in mind that none of this; not you, your employees, your brand, or your business, is going to change in a major way in just a day. Becoming a Christian business leader is a journey. You just need to get started one new day at a time, one new decision at a time, and one new conversation at a time. Even a one degree shift in direction (which feels small) can create a very different destination for you over time. I think the real power in this book will be revealed over time as you and your business grow. You will definitely be able to act on some of these practices today. Other things may not feel relevant to you until a few years down the road. That's okay! God will reveal it all to you in time.

In part one, you learned about building a solid foundation for your life as a Christian business leader. In part two, you learned about how to build the framework of a successful business. In part three, you learned how to build the business itself. You'll be working on each part every day, and improvements will be made as you apply it. Don't feel like you can't move to part two or three until you master part one. None of us will master part one this side of heaven. That's one of the reasons we need grace in this life. However, don't skip working on part one in an excitement to build parts two or three faster. Without God as your foundation, you may find that you are not really pleased with the business you are building.

In the introduction of the book, I shared that I grew up in poverty. I didn't share that I was severely bullied including receiving death threats, and I didn't share how alone and worthless I felt as a kid. This insecurity is one of the reasons that I believed money and power could fix my life. After I graduated from high school and moved out, I started to pursue money. Once I got into sales and saw how much money you could make, I was hooked. I wanted to do just about anything (as long as it was legal) to get that money and power so I could finally feel valuable. That was my pursuit.

Looking back on my life, I see how Jesus was always pursuing me. None of us can outrun God forever. He loves us too much to lose us in eternity. He sends new opportunities to every human being every day of our lives in various ways to know Him and be known. New invitations to repent, confess, find forgiveness, and follow Him. People always wonder about the remote villages of the world who don't know Him yet. Can God still reach them if missionaries can't get to them? I think He can. I think He can use dreams or a myriad of other things to get their attention. We certainly have a part to play, but He is the one who pursues us with or without human participation. We're not the hero in the story. I didn't always see it like that, and many of my close friends and family don't believe in Jesus yet. That's okay. I believe He's still pursuing them.

God eventually got my heart and showed me that He was all I really needed. Everything else is just a gift and an opportunity to serve Him while we live our lives. We never know how many days we have left, so I no longer worry about money or titles. God is my provider for both of those things. I still have to work hard, but He's the one that gives me what I need. Now I am free to pursue the Kingdom in whatever job I do.

Here are a few things to think about as you work towards these things.

Staying Motivated - all of us will face setbacks and discouragement, but God remains faithful. We only need to be reminded of His past goodness and the call He has placed on our lives to start to feel that motivation again. This is where your church family and loved ones can step in to be an encouragement.

Avoiding Distractions - with a real enemy who uses this tool regularly, distractions will be everywhere. That's one of the reasons abiding in prayer is so important. Stay connected to the Father. Plan your work and work your plan. Eliminate things that are getting in the way.

Building Habits - habits take some time to build or be replaced. Keep the habits you'd like to have in front of you as much as possible to remind yourself that you've decided to do a new thing! Also, get a friend who can be an accountability partner for you to help you build those new habits.

Correcting Opportunities - there always seems to be plenty of things that need to improve, and you may not be able to get it all done in the time frame you want. The best solution to this is to identify the ones that must change immediately while turning a blind eye to the rest temporarily. Don't worry! They'll still be there when you've fixed those immediate things. It's a process.

Celebrating Progress - last but not least, take the time to celebrate the wins! It's very important for everyone involved and puts fuel in the tank for the next challenge. People often feel like they are too busy to celebrate, but I would argue that it will help your team overcome the next challenge much easier. Personally, I love to celebrate by having team dinners! Some teams go to sporting events while others just have doughnuts in the break room. It doesn't have to be a big thing; it just matters that you celebrate. Also, make sure you take the time to thank God for what He is doing and what He has done!

What's next? That's between you and God. He will show you where to go from here. Where ever it is, I'd love to hear about it by email at **acsouthsmith@gmail.com**. Send me your comments, feedback, and stories. If you have any questions, I'll try to respond. Until then, I want to leave you with one final Big Idea and the summation of this book. Never forget that God has set you free, that you can walk in freedom, and that you can pursue who He has created you to be. I believe the best is yet to come!

Blessings my friends,

Adam

Big Idea:

God pursues us, so we can pursue the real life He intended for us. This is The Pursuit.

Acknowledgements

There are so many people that pour into us throughout our lives, and we don't usually thank them enough. I have stopped believing in the "self-made man/woman" and started believing that we all benefit from the people who believe in us. I wanted to take a moment and thank a few of these people who have meant everything to me.

To start, I want to thank my Lord and Savior Jesus Christ, because my real life is found in Him. I want to thank my wife and kids. My wife is a hard-working, talented, and gracious person, and she's my best friend. She is an amazing leader. I couldn't imagine doing this life without her. My kids are the best present anyone could ever get, and I am so proud of each one of them. I want to thank my mom for all her sacrifices over the years doing her best to put food on the table. I want to thank my dad who used to look down on me from the bleachers but now looks down on me from heaven. My dad was probably my biggest fan and taught me that people are more important than money.

I want to thank my brother, sister, brother-in-law, mother-and father-in-law, and extended family for showing me what it means to love one another. I want to thank my friends for their continous support and encouragement. I want to thank all of my bosses and co-workers who put up with me over the years; especially when I wasn't always easy to lead. I learned so much from each and every one of you.

There were a few people who helped me make this book better; my good friends Jeremy Alexander and Tish Holmes. These heroes of mine are truly selfless friends.

I also want to publicly thank the people at my church,

newlife, and all the brothers and sisters in Christ I met along the way in my travels to St. Kitts, Stillwater, El Paso, and Las Vegas. Specifically, I want to thank Jeff Costello; the man who baptized me and discipled me as a new believer in Christ. I want to thank my friend and pastor, Wes Davis, for his guidance over the years and patience in receiving a LOT of emails from me. I also want to thank my friend and mentor, Dan Serdahl, who helped me understand that Jesus loves me far more than I realize.

This list wouldn't be complete without listing some of the other people who made an impact in my life. Here are a few of their names:

Mrs. Reed - 4th grade teacher
Oliver Hanley - 5th grade teacher
John Callaghan - basketball coach
Xavier Miranda - basketball coach
Greg Leach - math teacher
Jennifer Lee-Wilkins - art teacher
Steve Blacksmith - basketball coach and YL leader
Ms. Murphy - DECA teacher
Carl Olson - drama teacher
Chris & Danna Olsen - basketball coach and P.E. teacher
Tom Diefendor - manager and first mentor
Harlan Stewart - manager and friend
Aaron Capps - owner of Advantage Nissan
Shane Edwards - manager and friend
Mark Clark - manager and Christian mentor
Scott Jones - manager and mentor
Bryan Stanley - manager and mentor
Rick Elkins - friend and mentor
Ron Youtsey - friend and mentor
Eric Roberts - friend and mentor
Phil Daubenspeck - manager and brother in Christ

About the Author

Adam C. Smith was born April 28, 1979, in Arlington, WA. He graduated from South Kitsap High School in 1997, The Art Institute of Pittsburgh Online Division in 2009 with a Bachelors in Media Arts & Animation, and Western Governors University in 2018 with a Masters in Business Administration. Adam spent the better part of the first ten years of his career in sales and sales management roles working for car dealerships selling new Toyota, Subaru, Chevrolet, and Nissan vehicles. He spent the next ten years in various retail management roles with companies like Linens N Things, Target, and Starbucks.

Adam became a Christian in 2002 and felt a call to pastoral ministry early on, but he did not step into the call to paid ministry roles until 2017 when he became a Kids & Families Lead at his church. In May of 2019, he joined West Sound Youth For Christ as their Juvenile Justice Ministry Area Director, and he was promoted to Development Director a few months later where he serves today. He also spends two Sundays a month at a local nursing home providing the sermons for their chapel service.

Adam loves art, basketball, swimming, cooking, all things business, and Christian theology. He lives in his hometown of Port Orchard, WA, with his wife and children. He loves their small community and has volunteered in various ways to make it a better place.

In 2015, Adam started his first business, Blue Creations, to be able to use his artistic skills to help others. Adam provides a variety of art, graphic design, branding, and consulting services.